Eskiboy

Eskiboy
Wiley

WILLIAM HEINEMANN: LONDON

1 3 5 7 9 10 8 6 4 2

William Heinemann
20 Vauxhall Bridge Road
London SW1V 2SA

William Heinemann is part of the Penguin Random House
group of companies whose addresses can be found
at global.penguinrandomhouse.com.

First published by William Heinemann in 2017

www.penguin.co.uk

A CIP catalogue record for this book is available from the
British Library.

ISBN 9781785151590 (Hardback)
ISBN 9781785151606 (Trade Paperback)

Plate section designed by Dinah Drazin

Typeset in India by Integra Software Services Pvt. Ltd, Pondicherry

Printed and bound by Clays Ltd, St Ives plc

Penguin Random House is committed to a sustainable future for
our business, our readers and our planet. This book is made
from Forest Stewardship Council® certified paper.

For Richard Antwi

Contents

Introduction

I hate bullshit books. I've read a lot of biographies. Most of them are boring. I don't want to put out the same old story: 'Oh I grew up on an east London estate, mans was getting shot every week, rah rah rah.'

It's no use trying to make yourself look good, or better than you are. People know straight away when you're not being authentic. I always say I need everything to be as real as it possibly can be – even if I come off worse because of it. The best books are like films: you read it, and you feel like you can see it. You've got to be able to see it.

It's stupid to stick to one story. How can anyone have just one story? My sister will tell you I'm four different people. You all know me as Wiley, the wickedest grime MC, jumping on stage going apeshit, popping off on Twitter. There's Richard, the boy following in his father's footsteps, climbing out of his crib to bang on the drums. There's Kylea, the lost kid, the wildchild who had to learn how to become a father. Then there's Godfather, the don who was there at the beginning, and is there still.

And beyond them all, there's Eskiboy, who I can't even really explain. The boy who likes to help people, but has coldness in his heart. Who'll you probably have to read this book to understand.

I can't tell these stories on my own. I don't even think it would be my story if it was just me telling it, so you'll also hear from those people with something to say, including my best friends from early, some of the best MCs of today, the people who really know grime music, the people who have taught me something and who I respect, and the people who might know me better than I know myself.

This is my life, my highs and my lows, but it's not really about me. When I make music, help the scene or even do something like this it's like I'm not alone any more. It's like I'm doing it for people like me. For people who grew up like me. I'm doing it to help people who are lost like me.

Part One
Richard

1. Growing Up

Richard Senior

I lived in Limehouse when I was growing up, but I went
to school in Bow. East London back then was nothing
like it is now. It wasn't the safest place in the world,
but it was home. There was a real sense of community.
Everybody knew everybody. I mean, I was one of eight,
and we had extended family everywhere.

I was the only one to go to school in Bow. And that
was how I met Kylea's mum. She was the sister of one of
my best friends, Junior. So I used to go and see Junior
a lot where they lived, in the Isle of Dogs, or what was
called the Isle of Dogs back then, and just got to know
the family. They used to come over to see my sisters. It
went from there. We just met up, really. We got married
when I was twenty-two.

I was in a band called Tribe at that time. The band
was good, but it was a lot of work. We didn't have much
money, so we had to make do with what we had. We
were booked to do a gig in Gravesend once, but when
the day came we realised we had no car, and these
massive speakerboxes. Everyone said no, we can't do
it, we've got speakerboxes. But I said yes, we can, let's
just get the train. So we carried the speakerboxes to
London Bridge, got everything on the train, carried

them to the venue, wired them up, did the gig, and then had to carry them home again. That was how it was. But the shows were electric. Grabbing the mic was commonplace. Everyone wanted to be the best, everyone wanted to do their thing. Competition was fierce. There was a real energy to the music. I loved it.

Then we moved to Kent. The band kept going. Every Sunday, or nearly every Sunday, we'd be jamming. That's all I did. Jamming and listening to music. I liked heavy bass, hard-hitting music. At that time, as a Rasta, it was about dub, it was about reggae, soul, Motown. Maybe some new jack swing. I listened to a lot of music. There was always music in the house. A lot of tapes, a lot of vinyl, but also a lot of playing. Footsie's dad had a sound system called King Original. There were a few other sound systems that we listened to, when we went to dances and that.

I was in my early twenties when I had him. It kind of changed me in a lot of ways. Everything started to change when I brought him home. I named him Richard, but soon we all started calling him Kylea. Kylea is his mother's name for him. Might have had a couple of rums ... We've got like little nicknames for him as well. My mum calls him Kylea or Kat.

For the first few years or so, I kept going with the music. His bedroom was our rehearsal room. Or our rehearsal room became his bedroom, when we brought him home. My son had his cot in the corner, and that was it. Sometimes we'd leave him in there while we were playing, not loud, you know, and I used to watch him. He always used to listen, listen to what we were doing. Even when he was a baby, he was paying attention. And one day he climbed out of his cot and came over to the drums, started banging on them.

As a child he was very inquisitive, very sharp, very helpful. He didn't like any form of disappointment. If he knew you were trying to do something, he would help you, without even thinking about it.

I made a set of headphones at the time. The headphones I was using weren't heavy enough, bass-wise, so I made my own out of some small speakers. I wanted maximum bass, but clean, you know. They were good. They used to make your ears hot. Sometimes I'd catch him with the headphones on, listening along with the music. Or I'd see him touching the keys on the piano, trying to find melodies, trying to find something.

Music was kind of our thing, really. The band used to rehearse down in Tunbridge, and I used to take him with me, religiously. And whenever me and his mum had a little fight or something – nothing serious, you know, just the usual arguments – I'd get him and go off to rehearse. It was a nice adventure.

*

That all ended really when I had a disagreement with his mum one day, and she threw my guitar out of the window. That was a wake-up call for me. I wasn't making any money from music, and not really doing anything that was going to get me money in any real way, so I had to decide at that time whether I was going to continue with the music, or go for a conventional job.

I started looking for a job, and three came along at once. One was in a lighthouse. It was right at the edge of London, by the river, all the way down this narrow road. I got to the lighthouse and met the lighthouse keeper or whoever he was, and we had a chat. I can't remember what the job was exactly, but I think a large part of it was just sitting in the lighthouse. I mean, it would have killed me. He said, 'It seems like you're a little overqualified for this.' In the end, I took a job with British Telecom, and moved back to London.

2. Making Music

My very first memory of music is my dad playing his bass guitar. I think we were living in Kent at that time, and he must have put on a video, probably an old reggae video, a show like Sting or whatever. I remember watching the show, watching the drummer, watching the singer, and watching my dad playing along on his guitar, this heavy reggae bass line. I was interested.

Music was always on when I was growing up, at least when my dad was around. I wanted to play too. So one day, my grandparents ordered something big from Ikea or wherever, and they had all these cardboard boxes lying around. I just started banging them – putting them together and banging them. That was the beginning, really. Making a drum kit out of boxes. But I was really young, I didn't know what I was doing, I just liked hitting them. My grandparents let me keep the boxes in my room, and at night I'd climb out of bed and go and bang them until my grandparents came in and told me off. And that was my first attempt at making music. I was like two or three years old.

*

When I was five or six, my dad bought a real drum kit.
I was always in the studio, just wanting to copy what I
saw him and his mates doing.

At that time he was in a band with some of his
friends. Footsie's dad, for example. I think it was his
drum kit actually. But they also had a piano, guitars,
speakers. They were sick musicians. They'd play little
hippie festivals and whatnot – they didn't blow up, but
they were good.

I was never really properly taught, but I used to pick
up the instruments, have a little go on the piano, have
a little go on the drums. Learning slowly, until I could
play something on them all. The band used to go to
Tunbridge Wells and practise and stuff and sometimes
they'd bring me along. It was all live. I'd just sit in the
corner and watch them, but after they'd played for a
while my dad would jump on the drums and say to me,
'Right, go on, show me some chords, kick it, kick it.' So
I'd play the piano, or play the guitar, try and keep up.

Music was fun, but it was also supposed to be a form
of punishment. Whenever I did something bad, my dad
would take me and sit me in a corner, tell me to practise.
The first time it happened I remember it felt like a
punishment. After that it was just fun. Just jamming
with my dad.

3. Fight Night

I don't really have many proper memories of my childhood. I remember living with my nan, being in Kent. But for the early years, not much.

I remember school, and playing football. I loved football. I've been a Tottenham fan my whole life. I remember being about five or six, at primary school, and I'd made a friend who had a little Tottenham shirt with 'Holsten' in tiny writing across the front. He was the one who got me into it properly, when I was buying my first football boots and that.

I used to play as a winger – I knew what to do, scored a few goals and that – and you know what? I reckon I could have been a pro if I'd moved to London a bit earlier. Because in Kent, I was absolutely a baller. Then you get to London where all the pro clubs are, and the kids are just gonna be sick, aren't they.

What I didn't know at that time was that making it as a footballer is all about who you know, and who loves you. It might be cos you're the manager's son, or you're related to someone, that you'll get those trials for Leyton Orient. Or you'll find a coach who'll go to the ends of the earth for you.

I went to Gillingham for trials, and there were some really good players there. The level of football was high for me. But it's not the same in Kent, without Chelsea, Arsenal, Tottenham, West Ham. There's just Gillingham, and loads of semi-pros. There's no comparison with London really.

*

Other than football and school, Kent for me was more sounds and sights than anything else, you know? TV especially. Cartoons, sports. Computer games. I always knew where the fun was.

I remember going to the arcades with my family. Playing *Street Fighter. Ridge Racer. Streets of Rage. Time Crisis. Out Run. Tekken. Virtua Fighter.* I loved the noises from the computer games. I loved everything about them. The first time I got paid, I went to the arcades with about £1,000 and spent it all.

And boxing. Oh man, I miss all those old fights. Mike Tyson on TV, early in the morning. Larry Holmes, Tony Tubbs, Michael Spinks, I think. My nan used to say, 'Go to bed,' but I'd just sit there, on the floor of our front room, and she'd let me stay up. She knew that it meant a lot to me. They were always weird times. I'd be struggling to stay awake, but excited that I was allowed to stay up. Sometimes I'd fall asleep on the sofa and wake back up in a panic. But when the fight started – boy!

That was the best. One of my favourite childhood memories. Tyson. He was the king.

4. Kent

My mum's brother Junior was murdered in an argument just up the road from where my nan lived in London. Stabbed twice. The first thing Nan did afterwards was to move us all to Kent. We were young, we didn't even really know what happened. Junior and my mum were so close, not just in age, but as siblings. And Junior was my dad's best friend. He was the one who introduced them.

Kent at that time was backward, like a million years behind London.

It was so racist that my sister came home from primary school one day saying that an Indian boy had called her a Paki. I was like, 'What are you talking about? There are loads of white people here. He's Indian. We're black. We shouldn't be racist to each other!'

Kent was just too slow for me. In London there are so many different cultures, so many different people, that race isn't really an issue. Even though I was quite light as a kid, it was hard suddenly being one of the only black boys somewhere. I stuck out like a sore thumb, and no kid should be made to feel like that. It was confusing. Kids shouldn't have to feel different.

5. Troublemaker

Janaya

One of my earliest memories of Kylea was when I was really little. Mum was looking after us and had taken us to her workplace in Lewisham. And he was one of those kids who just can't keep still. He was bored out of his mind, and moaning that he wanted to leave. 'Mum, I want to go home. Mum, I don't wanna stay here. Mum, how long till you finish?', that kind of thing.

Then when she wasn't looking, he turned to me. He had a stapler in his hands – he said it was magic and to see I had to put my finger in it. And when I did he bashed it down, and I got a staple stuck in my finger! I screamed the whole office down and Mum came running. He insisted he didn't know what it was, that he hadn't meant for it to happen. But we did get to go home, so ...

We always used to play pranks on each other. I was just as cheeky as him, but I'd always end up crying first.

He was always causing mischief, and he was always a risk-taker. I remember we were playing at my cousin's house in Limehouse once, just behind the basketball courts. What happened was they were doing weights in the garden for money, to see how much they could lift, and they said, 'Right, go on then, you have a go,' and I beat his friend, so I got some of the money. I don't think he was very happy about it. He had a little knife and started playing the game where you spread your fingers and stab the knife quickly between them, back and forth. He did it very fast, and then said I should play. I put my hand out and he started stabbing between my fingers, then went a bit faster and stabbed me in my hand. I don't have the mark any more, but I remember it.

We didn't get up to much trouble in Kent. Kent was basically all white. It's changed a bit now, but there weren't many black people at all in Kent back then. There were a few Asian people, maybe, but that was about it. And it was racist. I used to get quite a bit of abuse, name calling, things like that. On the streets occasionally, but mostly in school. But they didn't really bother Kylea. He was very popular in school. He was the popular kid. He had a bubbly personality, he was a good character. He could talk to anyone. And I think he started rapping back then – which must have been quite a new thing in Kent. But it was mostly because he was so good at football. The best, in fact. And everyone knew it. It's a bit weird, isn't it. He was good at football, so he was popular, so people didn't pick on him. But they did pick on me.

I remember my nan was working crazy hours at the time. She wouldn't get home from work until like one or two in the morning, and was up again at six or seven to get ready to go back. She'd always wake us up in the morning, make sure we got dressed and ate breakfast, and for a long time she walked us to school together. Then she'd run off to work. I think she was actually supposed to start at seven or eight, so walking us to school must have meant that she was always late.

That all changed when Kylea started playing football. Suddenly we had eleven different boys ringing our bell every morning, like, 'Is Richard ready to go to school?' At first my nan was angry: 'Why do these boys keep coming to our house? Tell them to go away!' But then she must have realised that we'd be safe walking in together, so she welcomed them in. We'd be eating breakfast, the boys would arrive, they'd come and wait in the hall, and then when we were done she'd shoo us all out of the door.

6. Back to Bow

Richard Senior

I was in Kent for six or seven years, until I got a job with BT. I moved back to London. Kylea and Janaya stayed with their nan. They were going to school down there, so it made sense that they stayed.

I used to go and visit a lot. Most weekends, or whenever I had time off. They seemed happy for the most part, at least while they were still quite young. But then one day I went down to see him and he said he wanted to leave. I remember it so clearly. He must have been about ten or eleven. And he was upset. He said, 'A kid deserves to be with one of his parents. I have to be with one of you.' So I said, 'OK then. Get your stuff.' Fair enough, I thought. 'But I warn you, it's not going to be easy.' He got his stuff, I put it in the back of the car, and brought him back to London.

I had no plan. I didn't know how I was going to manage. At that time I was used to just going to work, coming home, going to work, coming home. I was working strange hours, sometimes away for a day or two. So having to cater for a young man, without any backup, was kind of hard.

Having extended family helped, because he was close with his cousins. That was the linkage really. He was friends with them, and then he got to know their friends. I had to apply for secondary schools. He got into my old school in Bow. I don't think they knew what to do with him. School was good for him because he was starting to meet people like him, people with the same tastes, the same talents, the same drive, and they could put something together. But school wasn't so good in other respects. Music was really the only thing. Music was the only thing for him.

It was a difficult time for all of us. But it was when he came to London that he started making friends, meeting people who had the same kind of vision that he had. Because they were all school friends together.

I was still making music. A lot of my spare time was focused on music, rehearsing, making tracks. Or just playing music. He was still interested, and he was beginning to learn a lot for himself, from watching me, or asking me to show him how. He was a quick learner. Everything from bass guitar and drums to the early computer programs. I had a little set-up in the corner, and he would play around with that. We still listened to a lot of music as well, a lot of dub, reggae, soul, whatever was hot at that time. I remember playing him 'Strange Fruit' by Billie Holiday, and trying to explain what the song was about to him. He was a bit young at the time – he didn't understand it. He said it sounded scary. He liked 'Golden Brown' by the Stranglers, and quite a lot of classical music as well. I love Vivaldi, so I remember us listening to that quite a bit. He always used to listen to music a lot as well, independently of me. He just soaked it up.

The hardships and struggles at that time were the usual struggles: money, the streets. Even then, not really being safe. People hustling. There were still people trying to lean on you for whatever reason. But I come from a big family unit, so everybody was there: his uncles, his aunts. There's a lot of respect and love there.

He got himself into little scrapes. Imagine just trying to feel your way around, having come up from Kent. He would have to explore the streets, as it were. Seeing what's out there. But I tried to keep him as busy as possible. I didn't want him roaming around. From my point of view, he's always been a caring young man. But obviously you don't see everything that goes on. He would probably give you some darker stories.

It was just me and him. And we had our disagreements, just like anyone else. We got into little wrestling matches or whatever, but we would never argue for long. Deep down, our bond had always been about music. We'd listen to music together, make music together, and talk about music for hours on end.

7. Moving On

Janaya

We were in Kent together until I was like seven or eight. It was just me and Kylea and my grandparents. My mum and dad would come and visit after they split up, but it was just us really. Kylea went through all of primary school down there. But he wasn't happy. Or he was happiest when my dad would stay. He couldn't understand why we had to live in Kent when our parents were elsewhere. I wasn't happy either, but I was too young to question it. I didn't know what the alternative would be.

It all changed when Kylea was ten or eleven, I think. My dad was visiting and Kylea just asked if he could go and live with him. He wasn't angry so much, more upset. So my dad said yes, he would take him back to London. I wasn't happy at all. I was crying, shouting at my nan. She told me, 'He's a boy. He needs his dad.' I remember standing in the doorway saying goodbye to Kylea. He promised that he wouldn't be gone for very long. He said that Dad would come back for me.

So I stayed, and he left. It wasn't the same without him there. Even though it was just me and him, we still had someone, you know. I loved my nan but she was busy, and she didn't know me like Kylea. I was lonely.

*

I think I lasted three or four months. My mum was living in London again, and I called her up one day and asked her to come and get me. This was over the school holidays, in the summer. She picked me up just like my dad picked up Kylea, and took me to her place, in south London. A rough bit of Peckham. I loved my mum, but I didn't like it. And then someone got shot nearby. I moved back with my nan, and started primary school again in the autumn.

After a little while my mum came to live in Kent, too. She moved in with my aunt, who had a house a couple of doors down from us. My nan actually owned four houses on the same road. She ran a respite scheme for parents with disabled children. The parents would go off on holiday and my nan would take care of the kids.

I used to go and stay with my mum down the road occasionally, but I always went back to my nan's. I think I was just more used to the routine there. I started going to a local private school for girls. It felt like we were more of a family, although I didn't see all that much of Kylea then. He would visit with Dad, but not very often.

Things all changed again when I was about thirteen. Mum moved back to London, to Shoreditch. I went to visit and really liked it. It was lively. Completely different from Kent. My mum said I could move in with her if I wanted, and so I did. My mum picked me up and drove me to London. I started at Bishop Challoner on Commercial Road, a couple of miles from my mum's place. It was a shock when I moved back. I mean, we'd been taken to visit, knew people there, had lots of family in London, but it was another world.

The best thing about it was that Kylea lived five stops down the road. Suddenly I was seeing him all the time. He'd come and stay with us for a bit, or I'd go and stay with him. In Kent we were set apart. And when we moved to London we were set apart. We were two young people who'd popped up from the middle of nowhere. But he was finding his feet. The music was beginning to take off, or at least he spent most of his time making music, or with his friends from Bow – Danny, Target, all of them. I knew a lot about music from my parents, and from my dad especially, although not like Kylea. This was a whole new world.

That was another good period for us. We all got on, even Kylea and Mum. They didn't even really bicker. That's the thing with them: they're nice to each other most of the time, but then will have one huge fight and promise never to speak to each other again. The next day they'll talk on the telephone and sort it all out. It will never last long.

8. Inner City Life

'Infants, Juniors, College, University, bowl of porridge.
Served with toast if you like, butter.'
Can I Have a Taxi Please?

I would not be Wiley had I stayed in Kent. As soon
as I moved to London and got into secondary school
everything was just easy. Bow was amazing. All the
kids were funny as hell. I wasn't that cheeky myself, I
just kept my head down. I liked working, looking back,
although at the time I wasn't sure I did.

I had to make a lot of big decisions from early on. I
was independent from early on. I wasn't a bad kid, but
I was just a bit lost. I was easily distracted. There was
a lot of road stuff happening, but I always had respect
for human life. I avoided all the street drama – all the
running and chasing and beating and stabbing.

It wasn't just related to poverty. It was kids with only
one parent, or kids with no parents, no role models.
It was always the kids who went through the deepest
shit that had the greatest energy. And they can use it
in different ways. They can use it for good, if they have

someone to show them how. If they don't, it can lead to jail, or to violence.

Back then, I realised quickly that a loss is sometimes just a loss. If you're caught up in any violence or drama, you think that if you take a loss, you have to go out and get a win. That's the way the world is. But sometimes you have to let it go. Use the energy you have for revenge and channel it into something you enjoy doing. That energy can be cold like ice, and people can get hurt. You just say, 'Nah, I'm not having it,' and people go to jail, or people get killed. Or the energy can be hot, and you can succeed. That energy can take you all the way to the top. Don't move backwards, move forwards. Get on with life. Luckily I found a way to use the energy I had productively.

9. Family

Richard Senior

Back in the day they all used to play a lot of football. This was before the music really took over, when they were about thirteen, fourteen, fifteen, although there was a time when they were doing a bit of both. Anyway, all the boys used to get together and play tournaments in Poplar. Not tournaments as such, but they'd sort themselves into teams, your crew against my crew. No mixing.

Kylea had a good crew. I remember that Tinchy in particular was very good. They took it seriously too. I remember going down to watch them once, and they asked if I'd be the referee. So I said OK, walked onto the pitch. A minute later, Kylea commits this terrible foul, and he says to me, 'Dad, you didn't see that.' Tried to get me to cheat!

They were tight at that stage. In pairs, first. The formation always came in the form of twos. I don't think I can remember anyone that was a solo act, first thing. It would have been strange. People weren't solo acts back then. First in twos, most of the time, and then a crew. Friends, football, but for him and his friends, music as well.

The music was quite a bonding experience. Like with football, they were all tight, but quite welcoming to new people, actually. If you could spit, you were picked up by someone. The bigger the crew, the better the crew, the bigger the following. And the following also had a lot to do with where you lived. So for us, we were supporting anyone from E3. That's someone who was from the ends, you know. An E3 soldier.

Kylea was always encouraging. He'd push people to take the mic, he'd listen, and if he thought they were good, he'd bring them in. Even if they weren't good, he'd find something for them. Organising dances, DJing, helping with white labels.

The nice thing with all of this – the friends, the football, the crews – was that it was like we were a big family. Everyone knew each other in one way or another, either through family or friends. I mean, I was still friends with a lot of the guys I went to school with, they all lived in the area. And we were very close with our neighbours, and knew a lot of people nearby. I knew everyone's parents, you know, that's the thing of it. If I didn't know your parents I knew your uncles or aunties, if I didn't know them I knew your brother, if I didn't know your brother I knew your sister. If I didn't know your sister *my* brother knows *your* sister. All of Kylea's friends I knew in one way or the other – Danny Weed, Scratchy, Target. Kids you'd look out for. And the kids wouldn't just see each other at school, or at football, but at christenings, weddings, big family parties. Everyone would be there.

Family is important. We have a big family, so we know everybody. From my age going right the way down to my youngest brother. And that's how it was with the music. The same relationships continuing.

10. Wilehouse

*'I came to the game with knowledge and brain,
I came to the game with anger and pain.'*
The Game

We came from the ashes. It wasn't a war zone, but it was a bad place. Young people getting stabbed, people getting robbed, people with guns, people hustling, selling drugs, you name it. It was a kind of ghetto life, if you want to look at it that way. I'm from a council estate. I know what milk tokens are.

The area has changed a lot now. I think now it's really calm compared to what it was back in those days. The dynamics of the place have changed; there are different people coming into the area now – in Hackney and Shoreditch, Canary Wharf, and Tower Hamlets in particular.

But back then Bow was a place where things happened. People would come and hang about, buy drugs, just stand around and chat, especially around Roman Road Market. You had the youth centre, you had food, you had the trainer shop – DC's. If there was ever any beef or arguments, people would go straight to Roman Road Market because they know they'll be able to find certain people there. Back then, you couldn't really sit around on your own.

There was a lot of peer pressure, and no one to ask for help. My dad looked out for me, tried to keep me out of trouble, but when you reach a certain age you stop listening to your parents. Our teachers didn't really understand us. At school it was 'Do it this way' or nothing. Not all of us were cut out for exams and university. So we had to just do our thing.

Saying that, there was the occasional teacher who'd pay attention, who'd spot something. Teachers who believed in raising people up rather than trying to tick the boxes. Someone who can listen, even on the bad days. That's what we needed. Someone to listen on the bad days.

We lived in Bow, but used to spend a lot of time around there – Poplar, Stratford, Limehouse. Limehouse in particular. Limehouse was my cousin's area. But they used to call it Wilehouse, or like Wile Out, because of me.

What's gwaning, Nan? Y'aright?
Yeah, it's Kylea. What's gwaning, what's gwaning?
Yeah I know, Nan, I know you always tell me come out of
    London
But I can't. I am London

Ask London, I'm the grime kid
Nineteen for the first seventy-nine, I'm still alive with
More in store for the music stores
I'm hyping, on a mic ting
All day, we can spit all day
To the end I'm riding
The next ten years like a baby smiling
After them ten give me a black card
I've fly around the world buy two black cars
Too swift, too quick, can't see me, I ras
I'm powerful, and I got a powerful past
I'm London. I get praise in abundance

Have you ever wondered why I've never blundered?
A few slip-ups, otherwise I'm underground
I'm so London, everyting London
Ask anybody, anyplace, anywhere if Eskiboy represents
    London
I am London

You get what I'm saying, Nan? I'm out here
I'm doing this ting
Hold tight my uncles
Hold tight my grandad

You know what else, Nan? Listen

Yo, I'm the best in Bow and the rest should know
I'm the best thing since sliced bread
They can't test me, Nan, I'm the champion
So I suggest they run before they're dead
In this game, there's no time for mishaps
No time for Kit Kats, copper and lead
I don't see why everyone thinks it's a joke that I nearly
    ended up dead
Nan, see the bars I write, they got meaning
Can't test Boy Better Know, they're dreaming
Man might bust his head off the ceiling
When I'm in a race spraying bars I don't cheat, I deserve the
    wheeling
When you hear the name grime, Nan, I am the meaning
I brought my whole team in

And now it's a reality. There ain't no more dreaming

You get me, Nan? They're saying my name, like
Thousands and millions of people are saying my name
    around the world, Nan
That must be a good thing
I know you're proud
Eskiboy.

11. Lost Boy

Listen: people do not change. They get new ideas, they get new friends, they learn new things. But who you are is who you are. If you're a humble person, you'll stay that way. If you're wild as a child, that's who you're gonna be. Apples don't fall too far from trees. You're given one brain and that's it, you don't get a new one as an adult. I haven't changed a bit since I was a kid.

This story is quite obvious: my dad is the man. I'm the kid. My mum and him split up, and they both went where they had to go. My mum had to leave London when we were very young because she was going through some stuff. Her brother was stabbed to death. She probably hated London. I'm lost. I'm at my nan's, until one day I come to London. And the first day I came to London was the first day of me being Wiley, basically.

I never really saw what Kent was about. All I did was play football and then go back to the house. London was always in my head, so I never got that deep into it. I always felt like I was waiting for someone to come back and get me. So when I got back to London, I was like, 'Riiiiiight! This is my place!' I was born there, I'd go all the time to play with my cousins, so I knew that was where I was supposed to be.

My earliest and most important influence was always my dad. He was the strongest figure for me to see, and it's because he made me know that he was my dad. Even though he wasn't there every second, I thought about him all the time. I imagined what he might say. So whenever I went to try something, I would practise what I saw him do. I wanted to be just like him.

When my dad came and got me from Kent it was just me and him.

Then maybe a year or two later, he met someone new. It was a girl he'd always known, I think, but it was around that time they started seeing each other properly. It got serious, and she got pregnant, and then they had my brother, Cadell. It was good, but at the age I was, I couldn't really see it for what it was. Every time my dad was round at her place, I just thought, 'Oh, so he's round there. He ain't coming back, he doesn't care about me.' You know when you're young, and you're just angry. I hated her. Not in a bad way, but more because – it's my dad, innit? I didn't want my dad to be with some woman in her house. Is it jealousy?

But as I got older, I wanted him to be with a woman. I just want him to be happy. I don't want him to be sitting on his own.

I'm not a fan of step-parents. I'm not a fan of them at all. My mum had one or two boyfriends, but I never really friended up with them. Whenever that happened

I just went back to my nan's house. My mum didn't really understand. She was like, 'What do you think is gonna happen? If two people split up, are they gonna stay single for ever?' Do you know what I mean? 'They're going to move on, and find somebody that makes them happy.' And that's that.

Me and my mum are very similar. I feel at home when I'm in the middle of nowhere, and I got that from her. She couldn't sit still, she couldn't stop moving – she was going through a mad thing. Can you imagine? You've lost your brother at nineteen, and you've just had a baby. Having me and losing him came very close together. She didn't want to be around all those bad memories. She just wanted to get out.

12. The Patty Factory

Richard Senior

When Kylea was about fifteen or sixteen I set up a catering company with some of my friends. We made Jamaican patties. We hired a unit in Poplar Business Park, bought a load of machinery, and got started. The patty factory, we called it. We did it all ourselves. Because I was an electrician, I wired it all up. We had this huge oven, the size of a room, that kept breaking down, and I had to climb in and fix it.

I wanted Kylea there to help, to bring him into the business. Janaya too. This was when they were still at school, so they'd come in on the weekend, over the school holidays. Especially in the summer. There was always work to do. We ran it around the clock, pretty much. Go in at night and cook the filling, then roll out the pastry in the morning. We were making thousands of patties a day. It was getting quite big. Selfridges were stocking them. Harrods were stocking them. But we didn't really have the cash flow or the people to build it up. So we relied on family, on friends to come in and help.

We had a whole crew at one point: Danny, Target. But I had to fire them. They would throw my food around, mess about, not turn up. I think they had a flour fight once. So I'd fire them, but they needed the money, so they'd all come back, remorseful and saying sorry, and I'd take them on again. Fire them on a Friday, and they'd be back at work on Monday.

They helped out, don't get me wrong, but I don't think they ever really liked it. Kylea in particular. He'd turn up late, go home early. When my back was turned he used to put his feet up, pretend that he was the boss. This was when he was, what, sixteen, seventeen? The music was beginning to take off, but I thought working with me was a more sensible option. And then one day he just said to me, 'Look, Dad, I don't want to do this any more. I want to stick with music.' So I looked at him and I said, 'Well, God go with you then.' And that was that. The end of his only proper job, really. He's been making music ever since.

13. The Devil's Music

Richard Senior

Wiley's got it. There's a thing that we used to say: you don't necessarily need to play, you just need to understand what you're hearing and put it in some sort of order. Similar to the punk thing as well, because a lot of punk, early punk, they weren't really fantastic players, but they had something. They had the energy, the spirit, they went out there and they performed and that's very much the same as these guys. Very rarely would you find someone who's like a proficient player.

The best music is always ahead of its time. It will always go through a period of the public not liking before they start to like it. When jazz first came, people said it was the devil's music. Now it's an industry standard. But when it first came out: 'What they blowing those horns for? How comes they're using those? What's going on?' You know. And I think any genre of music that paves the way, whether it be drum and bass, garage, dubstep, has to come from somewhere, and it has to involve someone using their creativity.

14. Dubplate

My dad is all about music. That's his thing. And that's what's so unusual about us lot, as well. Our parents loved music, and our parents played music, and our parents all knew each other through music. It was kind of what connected everyone.

Their generation passed on a lot to our generation. For me at least, I'm doing what I'm doing because of them. He gave me the gift. They've paved the way, and we've reaped the rewards for their work. Maybe we've gone further because now it's easier to become someone with less work, do you know what I mean? It's not about playing instruments and singing. You can make a little tune and put it out yourself and have people pay attention.

We owe a debt to them, though. Not only our parents, but all the seventies, eighties reggae people, Tippa Irie, Smiley Culture, whoever, bro. These guys. We grew up listening to a lot of dub tracks. Dub was kind of what made us who we are.

My dad always used to say, 'I'm a roots and culture man. Anything that sounds good to my ears and my heart.' When they started out they all used to go to youth clubs. Everyone would come from different areas – Bow, Poplar, wherever – and try and get on the mic. Everyone knew who was good and everyone knew who was up-and-coming.

But you had to have bars. If you asked for the mic and you didn't have any talent, you wouldn't get the mic again. End of. The good people would get the rewinds, they'd get noticed. That's how it was with dancehall, with ragga and with reggae, back in the day.

The whole confrontation thing was exactly the same, too. Back then, if you jump on the mic, you've got to prove who you are. You couldn't talk nonsense, or just make something up. The bars that you were spitting were actually true. You had stories. That was really the start of MCing, or MCing as we understood it to be.

That culture also fed into jungle. Jungle knowledge is important.

Jungle was kind of the first music that we felt could be ours, or that we could be a part of. It was all happening in the early nineties, or up to 1995, 1996. I had just moved back to London with my dad, so I was around thirteen, fourteen, fifteen. A lot of people were into it. D Double E, Terror Danjah, Footsie, Slimzee. Getting decks, getting on the radio.

Slimzee and me went to the same school and we'd get the same bus home. I knew he DJed, and around the time I was getting into music myself. I remember having a conversation with someone else from school about him.

They bigged him up. And it turned out he lived across the road from me.

So one day, I went round to his house and asked if I could see his decks. He had all the hardcore selection already. And that was the music that was like clubbed into my brain at the time, fully. So I was gassed. I was like, 'Oh my god, I know that ragga tune!' I was really excited about any jungle tracks which had a little ragga sample or a hip hop sample. I used to love that, and had a lot of it.

Back then, it was all about the scene. There was a proper scene, and we were all trying to get into it. But we were all kids, really. We loved it, and they obviously showed appreciation to us for loving it, but we weren't really in it. Jungle kept it tight. Like they didn't care about major labels, they don't jump up for man, they weren't gassed about anything. They were feet-on-the-floor people. You can't just go in jungle and bust one tune then go clear. It didn't really work like that. You had to keep going and keep going. I respected them for that. Most other scenes are really disposable.

That was the start, in a way. It was the first time I realised that we could do this. We didn't really need anybody else. We had decks, we had the mic, we had the radio. Didn't need to wait for anyone, impress anyone, push anyone. Just us.

15. Kylea Part 1

Richard Senior and Janaya Cowie

Richard Senior: We lived in the pink block. Clare House. Next to Victoria Park.

Janaya: A few things happened around there.

R: Come on, we live in London. Things are always happening. But you know, it wasn't that bad. It was mostly kids running about, like they always do. Kids getting up to mischief. My dad always used to say, 'Manage your friends, manage your friends.' In other words, you're my friend, but it might not be a good idea for you and me to hang out. I know what you are, and you definitely know who I am. But we're still friends.

J: Yeah, you see that part of it a lot. Friends can often cause trouble.

R: He could head it off though. He's very open and very upfront and very direct. He's an honest person. He says what he thinks. There is no pretence at all. That's maybe why he takes things to heart so quickly. Like on Twitter. If someone says something negative, he'll act as if somebody's walked up to him and said it.

J: He's not as bad as he used to be, though. He is beginning to change as he gets older. He's getting used to it, or he can brush it off in a way that he couldn't before. And he is a little more careful about what he says, too. He's wary of offending people.

R: I think what he is starting to learn at this age is that everyone is entitled to their opinion, but that opinion doesn't always need to be heard. Sometimes it's being too open, or too opinionated, that can get you into trouble. It's sensible. But it's a shame in a way. I think that if you're an artist, when you're dealing with this music you've got to be able to take whatever is coming. So, if you're giving it and I'm giving it, it's like boxers, they go in the ring to hurt each other, they don't go in the ring to play. But afterwards, the chances of them saying, 'Well yeah, good fight,' you understand?

J: I think people said it was violent only because of the clashing part of it. That and the police. But there were only a few incidents that really got into a fight, do you know what I mean? He might clash with someone, but they're friends the next day, you know.

R: Yes, it never lasts longs.

J: There's always some friend. You would get a phone call and they would be like, 'Yeah, you know der der der.' You didn't really want to hear that. I remember being with him in Manchester, and someone rang him, I think it might have been Westwood, because they had heard he'd been killed, been stabbed to death. So he started messing with it. Letting his phone ring. He was getting ready for a show. Obviously more people are ringing now, because they can't get a hold of him. And then they start ringing me: 'He's dead!' And I was saying to them,

'No, he's not dead, because he's sitting here with me.' I don't know what happened. Someone put it on the old BBC website, they hacked the website and they put it on there.

R: I always worried about him. Not so much now, but back then, I worried all the time. I remember going to one gig, I think it was Sidewinder, maybe, and he's on stage with Titch and everyone. I go backstage, standing behind them, on the edge of the stage if you know what I mean, and I suddenly realise that something's happened. They looked a bit rattled, a bit roughed up. And then I look at him and see blood running down the back of his leg. He's been cut. But he was still doing it. So, when it comes to heart, I don't think there's too many people that have got as much heart as him.

Part Two
Kylea

16. Snare

I grew up with live music. That's why I'm quite surprised that I've turned into a computer bod. I can make a whole song from nothing, whether it's just instruments or whether it's sequences. We had to make something different. But my dad says he can recognise his music in what we make. He says he can hear himself. The drums are a big part of it. The snare, he always says. If you listen to any song from back in the day, it's the snare that makes it. The snare's important in grime. It's part of our identity.

I always wanted to be an artist, a performer. I'd watch Bob Marley, or MC Hammer, and think, 'Yes! That's where I want to be.' But also because I saw my dad do it. Even if I was someone's drummer or even if I was some small part of a group, or a collective, that would be enough, because I'd be following him. I've always wanted to do what I saw my dad do.

17. Wildchild

'You can't be weak to overcome this system we are in, you've got to be powerful.'
Doorway

In those teenage years, we were a crew. I was in Bow, but I used to go over to Limehouse. There was always a crew of us. We used to play football anyway, but then we started going raving, and saw what was happening with jungle and garage, and we started to get some ideas. A lot of people were DJing. Scratchy was DJing, Dizzee was too. Everyone was still on the decks.

We were into the music our uncles were raving to. More dancehall, more jungle. Early Prodigy, for example. Scratchy and Danny Weed had just finished school, and we started to come together. I was on pirate radio from the age of fourteen, fifteen. People used to encourage me: 'Come on Wiley, let's go on the radio.' 'Come on Wiley, there's a rave in Bethnal Green. Jump on the mic and I'll give you £30.' DJ Slimzee, for example. I think it was Slimzee who took me to my first show. We had to get a train there. I wasn't scared, though. By that stage I already had loads of A4 notepads filled with lyrics.

I could always tell the people who were good. That was my ability. We were friends, first and foremost. It wouldn't have happened if we weren't friends.

Those years were very important. They taught me how to help myself, but more importantly they taught me how to help others. That was the foundation. It was a training ground for what was to come. Maybe I was the training ground. I put time into people, helped them to get to where they needed to go.

I was like Ajax. Ajax train players. It's nuts. They put time into people, they work them hard. And then they sell them. They go on to bigger and better things. And that's what I have done. That's something that no other musician has done. Music is a big business. But I was just helping people. I didn't expect anything for it. I'm not saying I don't get paid, but I get paid for *my* talent. I don't take anything from them. I don't sell them. I'm like a Kung Fu master.

I helped people, and I don't expect anything for it. The problem is that no one can understand it. Money rules the world. We need it to survive. No can understand why someone would work, help, spend money, spend time, without wanting something for it. But I do get something for it. Maybe I wouldn't have been around for so long if I didn't do it.

18. Samurai

'Dad told me don't follow the herd
Instinct, yes, I follow the word.'
Can't Go Wrong

Every boy when he goes into the world has to find his own path. People show you stuff, both good and bad, and you need to decide what to do and what not to do.

I was very lucky not to go to prison. I knew what drugs were before I got into the game. There's a lot of money in drugs. Anyone who goes into it will find it hard to come out, because of the money. That's why people end up in prison. The risks go up as the money goes up. But drugs are not good, and that's it. Don't take drugs. Trust me.

I had a DJ friend who was a bit older than me, and he was really good at dealing. Not a gangster, just really good at it. And he pulled me in, and we started to make a lot of money.

I remember there was one guy who was quite regular. I was showing a new boy the ropes – how to look after the phone, do this, do that – and this guy called up. We go over, and he's got no money. So we're like, 'What now?' And he pulls out a samurai sword. Not a proper one, but a mini one. He started swinging it, walking towards us, so we ran. I thought I was fit, like I could run for long. But this guy didn't stop. He just kept going.

We escaped, but didn't really know what we were supposed to do next. I got a few of the mandem and we were going to go find him, but then my boss, the DJ, turned up and said no. 'We don't do anything to them,' he said, 'because they'll speak.' I think he sorted it out somehow. The drug game is a very dangerous game.

People got kidnapped, held for two weeks under the bed. People getting carjacked, people getting chased down the street. It's just street stuff. Things like that were going on all the time. That world is a bit dark. It can happen for any reason. This one doesn't like that one. If you associate with someone that someone else doesn't like, you can get dragged in. A lot of that happens.

The streets are crazy. No matter how bad you are, you can't avoid it. There are no rules. There's no ring, no boxing gloves. It's more dangerous than anything. You can get rushed by ten man, twenty man, thirty man. You can get shot, stabbed, hit with a hammer. Anything. Not just London, either. Anywhere.

In the end I had to cross a bridge. I had the record deal, and so I moved over to music. I could have kept on going with both, but that would have been greed. I stopped when I was twenty, twenty-one. I knew that I could do music.

19. SS Crew

Flow Dan

I'd known of Wiley from 1994, 1995. I used to listen to him on Rinse. Him and SS Crew. SS Crew was just a street group. Just mandem off the roads. People who went to the same school, grew up together.

I met him in 1996. I'm from Bow and Poplar, but because I went to school in a different area, our paths never really crossed. I did have run-ins with girls who talked about Wiley and the SS Crew, so I knew they were around, I knew they were close. But I didn't meet him until 1996, when they started at a college that was near my school. So we were like, 'OK, cool. So you're from Bow, I'm from Bow. We'll be getting the bus to and fro together.' And from there, we got to understand that we both liked music, and so he had time for me, in that respect. The relationship grew from there.

My house was the arena for watching sound system clashes. My parents had a load of videos and we used to watch them again and again. And then we heard the jungle MCs picking up elements of it: the charisma, the style of delivery, the lyricism. Jungle was a UK twist on that world. Up to that point there had been a lot of

US-influenced music, but jungle opened our eyes. It made us realise that our accents were allowed. Suddenly we could be ourselves. We didn't have to try and be anyone else. It made us want to do it.

We left college in 1997, and at that time, if you were making music, it was jungle, or drum and bass. Myself, Target, Wiley, loads of people who ended up in the Pay As U Go crew, were into jungle – playing on Rinse, going to shows, that kind of thing. Making music and selling a bit of weed. We were at the stage where we really should have been thinking about what we were doing with our lives. But we weren't, really. Wiley was though. He would say, 'Right, I'm going to the studio.' All of us were all like, 'Why? What for? What are you doing there?' He'd come back and play us these tunes he'd made, and we'd think, well they're shit, and not really care. But he persevered. He had something different about him. He wasn't the boss, but he was the most looked to, the most sought after, even then. We had another friend, who was a sick producer who did make it in the jungle world. DJ Trend. He helped Wiley.

If we were any bigger in terms of selling weed, the music wouldn't have taken off, because the two don't mix. It's impossible to keep them both up. If you do, you end up in prison. And we knew it. The beauty of being where we were from was that we grew up with criminals. There was no distance. We weren't worried about them, because most of the time the people to worry about were the people we grew up with. What's going to happen? Nothing. These people have known you your whole life. Obviously there would be one-off situations with one of your friends, but on the whole, it was comfortable.

20. End Product

Richard Senior

The earliest music that I can remember him being properly into on his own was drum and bass, jungle. He was a DJ, or wanted to be a DJ, but he started to spit on drum and bass tracks.

He started experimenting with music. I suppose there was a transition at some point from him spitting over drum and bass to creating his own music, and spitting over that. There was a tradition of that. At early house and garage raves you'd have people grabbing the mic to gee people up, encouraging them to feel good. That was their job, you know. But then all of a sudden, there was a change. People started grabbing the mic to tell stories. Grabbing the mic and having battles.

He always had a drive and vision. He's a good organiser. He can see the end product. That's the similarity we have. Even if someone's in the room and they're being negative, it's not about that person's negativity. It's about the end product. It's seeing the end product, and putting in the work to make it happen. You can say it's a gift, but in a way, it's kind of spiritual. It's like a connection you can make with someone.

He played a big part in forming those crews. He could hear someone, and know whether that person would fit.

We're going back to a time when there were more crews than individuals. It was about having four, five, six MCs in your crews. What voices could fit. And he was encouraging in terms of helping people write bars. He never wasted time in the studio.

It wasn't just with the music either. Not everybody could spit. But some people were good at other things. He would work out which people were good at what, and get them to help with things. But not in a bossy way, just making it all working. To get things rolling. Someone would be good at merchandising, another guy was good at drawing, another guy would drive. So Geeneus did one job, Flimsy was doing his thing, someone else was doing something else, you know what I'm saying? Putting dances on, you know. He helped everyone organise themselves to make this thing grow.

They blew up in east London before they blew up anywhere else. I think he was succeeding when he was selling the white labels. He was happy enough that the interest was there. I was happy that he was doing something. I was happy that he was enjoying the music.

21. I Don't Know What I'm Doing

If you're not going to enjoy the office job in the City,
then don't do it. Don't be chatting shit at twenty-six
about 'I don't know what I'm doing!' I don't wanna know
that. If you don't know what you're doing when you're a
kid, you're never gonna know. Meaning if you're a kid
and you want to be a footballer, or you want to be an
MC, or you want to be a DJ, nine times out of ten you
will become one. But if you wait till you're twenty-six
and turn around like, 'Oh no, what should I do now?' it's
too late. You've got to have an idea of what you're doing
when you leave school, when you're sixteen or eighteen.
At least an inkling!

22. Nicole's Groove

'Even when I done "Nicole's Groove" I couldn't see myself getting any credit, but I cropped up.'
Step 21

I'll tell you the truth here. Real grime was born from garage. From Heartless Crew, from So Solid Crew. If we had not listened to Heartless and So Solid, would we have created what we created? Maybe not. I think Dizzee's *Boy in da Corner* is a grime bible. I think *Home Sweet Home* by Kano is a grime bible. They're the first, before anything else. They steered us. But a big part of that sound came from garage.

Not a lot of people know this, but I started off DJing. I was called Wildchild. This is back in the mid-nineties. Before the Rinse FM days. I played more jungle back then, and people would come and MC with me – Breeze and that lot. But garage eventually took over.

Garage did all the deals. All the girls raved to it, so we used to go down to the parties to check the girls and whatnot. That's one of the first things that attracted us. Otherwise we probably wouldn't have gone. The biggest people on the scene were Heartless Crew, So Solid and

Pay As U Go, but also Paco and Plague, Major Ace, even Scratchy and Biggy were doing stuff. Imagine that.

Back then I was spitting bars, but I was into jungle, not garage. Garage for me was music first, lyrics second. MCs were there to hype up the crowd, give the shout-outs. In that way it's American on the sly, even if they're never gonna admit that. Heartless was something in between. Something new. They were the first people I heard mixing garage and ragga, and spitting on it. These were some of the elements that would go into grime.

Preshus MC was the first person to convince me that we could do it. Preshus was like the prince of garage at one point, bro! He was sick, like he had an army of fans and shit. He was the guy, and he showed me garage that was more MC-orientated. He was the one saying, 'Look at what So Solid Crew are doing! Look at what Heartless Crew are doing! We can do that shit!'

For a time there was this in-between sound. Maxwell D eventually became the leader of the garage scene for a while. He had the record deal first. He had that song 'Serious'. Very early, like 1999, 2000.

I was experimenting, playing around, doing a lot of pirate radio, but nothing big. Back then we were still learning. We were still dipping our toes. The Phaze One period was the beginning of coming up for me. Up to that point we'd all been bubbling along, but then I get asked to produce this track for Danny Sayer, Phaze

One – 'Nicole's Groove'. And it took off. This was Wiley
after Wildchild. It was something new. All of a sudden
it wasn't just me on my own, or me as part of a crew, it
was me and this person, so we just made a name – to
go forward together. It was like the very first stage of
getting it. 'Nicole's Groove' is a garage track. A classic
garage track, maybe.

I was still signing on when 'Nicole's Groove' came out.
The people who worked in the Job Centre were from the
area, so they were like, 'What are you doing? We've seen
you on the telly!' They signed me off. I was upset for like
a day, thinking, 'Oh shit, what if the music thing doesn't
come through?'

But to stay signing on would have been to stay in
their palm. They kind of did me a favour, it gave me the
energy I needed to get out. Get out of Wilehouse.

Sometimes people say you've made it, and you might say
thanks, but you know deep down that you haven't really.
Nothing will change. With this, people were saying
to me, 'Wiley, you've made it,' and for the first time, I
started to believe them. But I would also say, 'Yeah, but
I made it with Danny.'

And things were changing. There were a lot of other
MCs coming up at the same time as us. God's Gift, for
example. When he came through he was very young. He
wasn't even allowed in the rave one time. But he was
coming up quick. He was major. I remember he recorded

some key vocals early, the tribute track for example. He was on the path, he was with Pay As U Go as they were coming up, big money was being made. But then he was sent down. When he came out things weren't the same. He would have gone all the way, man. With those lyrics? He would have made it. It's not just me saying that. People in the record shops, people in the studios, they were all on him, do you know what I mean? And Kano was the next.

Grime wasn't there yet, but it was developing.

23. Wingers

'All the mums tell your daughters that Wiley's charming.
I'll wife her, while you're oohing and aahing.'
Welcome to Zion

The key to chirpsing at those garage raves back in the day? Have strong right and left wingers.

By the time garage kicked off, I was already Wiley. I had that reputation as Wildchild. As kids, we used to go to all the different estates to meet new people. So when we got to the raves and I was trying to draw a girl, nine times out of ten I would have already known her. In my day, you grew up with people before you started kissing them, or laying down with them. I had to wait for my day. I needed to be Wiley before that could happen.

It's like I had to develop my stage persona so I could stop feeling scared to talk to girls, who I thought were maybe too nice for me. I realised that girls like boys with confidence. Not the guy who's pissing around, who doesn't know what to say, who's giggling all over the place. Being known for doing something gave me a bit of courage to go up to girls, and know already that they wanted to talk to me. Suddenly you weren't worried about being rejected by that girl from round the estate, or the girl that everyone wanted to get with at school. I learnt to just sit back and wait for the girls to decide whether I was cute or not, and they liked that I wasn't overly trying.

I had a lot of friends who got all the girls in the first place. Danny Weed's brother Dominic, Target, Breeze – those guys were my wingers. They knew how to go up and talk to the prettiest girls, the kind of girls where you think, 'Woooooow, if I talk to you, you're just gonna walk off!' and be completely fine. They were so sick at that. I think they had grown into themselves a bit before me. Those guys could say to themselves, 'I'm a man. That's a girl. I'm gonna chat to her, and if she doesn't want to chat to me, I'm gonna walk away.'

I did try to use some stupid lines, I can't lie. I tried using lines from films, but then I realised that only works if the girl hasn't seen the film. The lines didn't matter. They could have been corny, or just saying 'Wagwarn, what's your name?' and it didn't matter because they could see who I was. They didn't used to rate me, but now they bigged me up! It gave me the confidence to just talk to them and be normal. It was great. Come to think of it, I network the exact same way now as I used to chirpse: 'Hi, I'm Wiley, where are you from? Let's exchange emails.'

Back then it used to be house phone numbers. You'd call up someone and their mum or dad would answer first and you'd have to go, 'Oh, hello, Mrs Blah-Blah!

Can I speak to Blah-Blah please?' Parents liked me because I was always polite. If they needed any milk from the shop I'd go and get it. They liked that I could come in their house, say hello and goodbye and hold a normal conversation.

Once they see that you're a respectful, reasonable person, the parents will only need to come and talk to you if something has happened and their daughter is upset. I've sat down on the sofa after I've had an argument with a girl, and her parents have helped talk us through it. A lot of rumours went around about me, but parents could always see that I was cool. No one wants anyone who's dodgy to be with their kid.

24. Blueprint

'Do you remember when I never had a tenner?
Out on the road at the end of my tether.
Gonna show up with the dough and watch them eyes get
redder.'
Terrible

Flow Dan

In 1998, 1999 garage came around. The mandem started
going to the Colosseum, West End, those kind of places.
Raving to that type of vibe. I didn't go, man was into
bashment. And it was different. It was a whole different
vibe, a whole different dress code. You had to slick up a bit
for those raves. I remember one time Wiley was like, 'OK,
you're not going? All right then. Lend me your shoes.' So it
was official. I couldn't go because Wiley had my shoes.

Central London at that time was renowned. You had
a lot of traffic there. A lot of girls. But anyone could be
there. We weren't there to get our names known. We just
wanted to draw girls, same as most young men. But a
lot of the boys just wanted to punch their way through to
fame. We weren't really up on gang culture. People used
to say, 'When you're going up West End, don't buck them
south London boys. Because they're on some gang stuff.'

We definitely got into fights, but it was usually with people we knew. It was never a postcode war.

Everyone started to gravitate towards the garage scene. Target wanted to DJ that sound now. There were girls in those raves. And Wiley was like, 'Yeah? There are girls in those raves? Let me hold the microphone.' Maxwell wanted to get involved as well. He was doing jungle with the mandem on Rinse anyway, but he was like, 'Yeah, there's a new sound. I want to do this.'

I remember watching *Top of the Pops* with Wiley and Target around that time, and So Solid were on. I was just like, 'Turn it off. It's not bashment. So there's a couple of mandem on the TV? So what.' And they were like, 'No! This is *mandem on the TV*! It's us! It could be us!' I think Wiley saw a blueprint of what to do. And so they started Ladies Hit Squad.

Around this time the other big crew was Pay As U Go, which grew from Rinse, and was mostly friends from our group: Plague, Major Ace, God's Gift, Slimzee. There were two separate groups for a while, Ladies Hit Squad and Pay As U Go, but the then owner of Rinse said to Wiley, 'You lot are getting a buzz. Let's work together, to make our team massive.' And that was a good call. I had a radio show of my own at Rinse at this time, me and DJ Karnage. My show was getting some good feedback, so I was rolled into Pay As U Go as well.

It worked when it worked. Pay As U Go was a strong team. In the UK you had So Solid, who were the stars. You had Heartless, who had the charisma and the longevity. They'd already been around for ages by this point. And then you had Pay As U Go. They were a mix of the two. We made So Solid music, but had Heartless charisma. You couldn't beat Heartless for charisma.

It was easy to be an MC around Wiley. I didn't really see the inside of a studio until Wiley took me there. And when I was there I was like, 'Shit, we're in a studio, about to make music.' But that part was easy. I remember driving home from the studio listening to the songs we had made and he was saying this is going to be one of many: 'This is going to help us go touring, to have a record deal.' I was like, 'Really? We sell weed! We can spit, and you can make beats, but we're quite successful at what we're doing now.' For the majority of us, we were thinking, all right, wherever it goes it goes. We were doing financial things that were feeding us, and the music was just a bit of fun.

A couple of months later, Wiley turned up with a tune, 'Know We'. It just took off, and became a sort of Pay As U Go anthem. Wiley was like, 'All right, but this is just the beginning. The next tune will be even bigger.' And that tune was 'Terrible'. That was me, Wiley, Jamakabi, Breeze. People were suddenly asking, 'Who's Flow Dan?' It was my first real taste of success. But I thought that was probably it for me in terms of my music career. I was having fun, but I didn't see where it would all go. I mean, we were making good money selling weed. It was Wiley and Target who encouraged me. They said, 'You can't stop. That's just stupid.' And so I kept going.

When Wiley took 'Terrible' to the shops, the shopkeepers were like, 'OK, so is this another Pay As U Go tune?', because it was a 'Know We' follow-up. But Wiley was like, 'No.' He was adamant. So the shopkeepers said, 'Well, what is it then?' He was cool just saying no for a while, but then his business sense kicked in. He came to me and said, 'So what shall we call us then?' I was like, 'Let's call it Pay As U Go. Why can't we just be one?' He was like, 'No. It needs to be different.' I don't really know why – I wasn't up on the politics that was going on between him and the powers that be at Rinse at the time. 'Rolling Deep' was a popular phrase in Bashment at the time. So I just said, 'What about Roll Deep? And entourage, not crew.' And he was just like, 'Yeah, that sounds sick. Let's go with that.' He trusted me.

Then the politics started. *I* started getting the calls now, because I was officially Pay As U Go, *and* officially Roll Deep. Roll Deep became kind of my show, with Wiley and Scratchy and others preferring to come in with me. We started to become a brand, making more music. And then when Dizzee arrived, that made it very hard for Pay As U Go. Business was being affected.

Wiley was the musical genius in both crews. He had the beats, the hooks, the sounds. And he couldn't be in two places at one time. Or he didn't want to be in two places at once. Before Roll Deep existed, if you wanted to book Wiley, which they all did, you booked Pay As U Go. It used to be that you booked the group, you got the star. But Wiley didn't always turn up. Promoters started to work out that if you booked Wiley, you got his group. You got Roll Deep: Flow Dan, Dizzee, everyone else.

Eventually he was like, 'OK. Pay As U Go, I've known you guys from school, from radio. But Roll Deep, you guys are my family.'

25. Uncle

Richard Senior

I was working a lot when the music really started. I wasn't around all the time. I remember I got home from work late one night, parked the van and walked up to the door of the flats. Outside there are all these boys, who stop talking and look at me, all respectfully: 'Hello, Uncle. How are you?' I nodded and said, 'All right, thank you,' thinking that it was a bit strange.

I walk over to the lifts and I see they're not working, so I start climbing the stairs. We were on the ninth floor. Quite a way up. As I'm walking up the stairs I bump into more boys on their way down. All of them stopped and said, 'Hello, Uncle.' I was just nodding along.

It was only when I got closer to our floor that I could hear the music. Seventh floor, eighth floor, getting louder and louder. I got to the ninth floor and there was another group of boys waiting at the top of the stairs: 'Hello, Uncle.' This time I wasn't having it. 'What's all this "Hello, Uncle"? What are you guys doing round here? Why are there so many of you?' I still didn't twig even when I got to the door. It was wide open. Music blasting. They had set up Rinse FM in the living room. DJ, decks, lots more boys. Someone hanging out of the window with an aerial. And Kylea just spitting.

I made some noise, but it's a difficult one for me. I believed in the music, and I believed in him. Maybe if he'd asked me beforehand I would have been easier on him. I love music. I'm not saying I would have said yes, but ...

26. Shoebox Theory

'Young black boy, too much money in a Nike shoebox, I am that one.'
Freestyle

Even before the *Treddin' on Thin Ice* days I was a big brother to the game. You could go to any record shop and see my name on the vinyl. People knew – that Wiley is Wiley, and if you don't know me, you don't know much.

I went quite quickly from making tracks on my dad's computer to doing it on my own. I used to go to Commander B's studio at first, and just lived there for a while. You know Commander B? 'Pum Pum Riddim'. He used to have a show on Choice FM. The studio was where Lethal recorded 'Pow'.

I was using the same programs my dad had on his computers – Logic, Fruity Loops. I liked playing instruments, but I saw people getting jobs done quicker on programs. By the time Logic and all those things came out, everyone was producing on computer. Fruity Loops was the one I made a lot of the early tracks on. It came with a standard 140 bpm tempo setting. You had to look for it to change it, you know, and I was just putting things together on there.

So we would go to Commander B's, Miloco in Shoreditch, London Bridge sometimes. Making new tracks, spitting, smoking weed, but all quite serious. After a while we began to look at how to expand it, how to take it further. There was this pressing shop in Stratford that my dad knew about, so when we had a track we were happy with, and had a bit of money from shows and that, we'd go there and press some vinyl. This was the beginning of the white label days.

I used to keep all my bars in a Nike shoebox in my bedroom. Everything I wrote I'd put in there, maybe throw out old ones, or switch them up. And then as soon as we started making money, like, real money, I put it in the shoebox. But it would never stay in there for long. Not because I spent it. I mean, I spent it, but not just on clothes and shit. I was DJing and was on the radio, buying records, spending my lunch money on records, starving. Not actually starving, but not spending money on food, waiting until I got home to eat and all that shit. I used that money to try and build up what we were doing. More equipment, more studio time. Setting up shows, promoting shows. Helping people out. I was investing it back in. The shoebox would be empty for a minute, but then I'd come back with more. My dad called it the shoebox theory. Use your money to grow. He did a similar thing with his businesses.

Record shops at the time operated on a sale or return basis. You dropped off your records, and went back a week later to collect the money and any records that hadn't sold. We could manage it between us at first, driving around east London in a van making drops, but pretty soon I had to rope in other people. I even had my dad driving around London picking up money. It was mad, bro. I was going to Rhythm Division, Total Records, Special Green, Black Market Records, all the record shops to be fair. I even used to go to Reading on the train to visit the record shop up there.

I think the tune that really stuck was 'Ice Rink'. We'd been making money before then, hearing our records get played at raves and on the radio, but 'Ice Rink' was a whole new dynamic. Suddenly record shops were like, 'We'll take it all,' handing over cash up front. And whatever else we had in the van. We couldn't keep up. 'Ice Rink' and also 'Eskimo' and 'Igloo'. We were selling thousands, bro.

'Eskimo' changed everything. My whole family were in on it – my sisters would spend all day putting stickers on the vinyl, and my dad helped drive the records around. It was a family business. We sold 10,000 copies and I thought, 'Rah! This ting is actually working right now. We've got to get on it properly now.' So we pressed that other tune, and ended up earning record label money before we even had a record label.

27. Success

Flow Dan

It wasn't that professional. Our intention wasn't
necessarily to have careers in music. Once we'd got
the mandem together and things were working in a
certain way it became the natural progression to take
things further, and take it seriously. But not everybody
in Roll Deep did. I was just happy being a team player,
and happy being part of the group. I didn't have the
motivation to be a solo artist, like Wiley or Dizzee.

Wiley is strategic. He's always had plans. He's always
had a bigger idea. Beyond the situations we were in.
When Wiley started to clock on that his instrumentals
had power, things changed. His beat-making started
to form the scene. What Wiley had was a hot sound, or
a sought-after scene that was growing by the day. And
there was a real demand for the music. Remember that
it was all underground at this point. You couldn't just
get it from anywhere. And he worked out how to use it to
his advantage. Back then it would cost £70 to master a
track, and £140 to press them up. £210. You could turn
that into thousands of pounds. He phoned me up one
day and said, 'Bring me £140.' He had money himself,
so I didn't understand why he wanted my money. But

I brought him the £140. And he said, 'All right, you've given me £140, here's 300 records. Here are the numbers to call. Go and sell them.' So you'd call up the record shops and say, 'I've got this new track by Wiley,' and that was normally enough. People would be going into the shop asking for his tunes, so they were eager to buy them up. They'd usually say, 'All right. I'll take ten.' Or 'I'll take fifty.' Sometimes a hundred. At £3 or so each. That £140 quickly turned into £600, or more.

*

The next stage was that he'd just give me music. He'd make music, and give it to me. He'd let me go and do it all myself. And not just me. Anyone in need. You didn't even have to be in the scene. Just call him up, 'Wiley, man, I need some records.' No one was doing this. No one gave their music away.

Some people say give to receive. But he just gives. And especially back then. It was just impulse. He'd say, 'I know you would do this for me.' Even if he didn't really know that person! He's generous. And generous with his time. If he thought you were good, he would help you. Say if he thought someone was a good MC. He'd say, 'All right. What are you doing with your life?' And the person would be like, 'Nothing.' And Wiley would say, 'Well I've heard you MC. You're a sick MC. You should MC.' And he'd take the person to the studio and they'd MC. He'd say to the next person, 'What are you doing with your life?' 'Nothing.' 'Well, you're an all right producer. You should produce.' And he'd get them set up. So he's just woken two people up to what they should be doing with their life.

The trouble was, when either one of these two people have some success, or want to speak to him about something, or ask for help, he might not pick up. They'll be like, 'Didn't you just tell me to do this? Now you're not speaking to me?' But it's not because of them. It's because ten other people are trying to call him, and so he's stopped answering his phone. He's not dealing with anyone. But he would never explain, and say, 'I'm not picking up because other people are causing me stress.' He just won't answer. When other things come into play, he prioritises them. Then six months later, he'll bump into the MC or producer again and he'll be like, 'You're sick!' And they'll be like, 'What? Are you messing with me?' But he's not. That's just how he is.

28. Wot Do U Call It?

'Goodbye to the man who don't like me
Goodbye to the woman who don't like me
Goodbye to the fingers pointing at me
Goodbye to the promoters that hate me
Goodbye to the people that's hassling me
Cos I'm sharp like a knife on the street.'
Wot Do U Call It

Grime is raw.

Grime started in the city. It started in the estates.
It started with people who didn't really have much. We
lived in one of the poorest boroughs in England. Don't
get me wrong, I grew up in a good area. It wasn't no
war zone. We were all brought up properly, we all went
to school, we all grafted. But it was gritty. We had drug
dealers, prostitutes, murderers on our doorstep. But we
also had Canary Wharf. We had something to aim for.
When you've got nothing, you have to strive.

Not all of us had happy family lives. Our world, back
then, was almost like another world. It was like we were
on another planet. Our parents, our elders, they had
their lives, their struggles, of course, but it meant that

we were kind of left to it. No one spoke for us. No one spoke to us. And I mean no one.

When it began it was an opportunity to talk about what we knew, what was happening to us, or around us. The sound came from our situation. It's a cold, dark sound because we came from a cold, dark place. These are inner-city London streets. It's gritty.

We tried to get into garage, which was big back then, but even the garage crews didn't want us. Everyone I looked up to let me down. We had no one to look up to. So we took what we had and we worked with it. Bits of jungle. Bits of ragga. Bits of garage. In the end we created something different.

You hear people talking about the grime sound coming from another planet? Well, that's because it does.

When it started grime was a young black man's punk rock. MCing is basically the same as singing in punk – shouting on a beat to say something. Shouting on a beat to get a reaction. The good thing is that grime is beginning to spread. The grime nationality is rudeboy, now. And anyone can be a rudeboy, you get me. It's not just for black kids any more. It's for everyone: black kids, white kids, Indian kids, Turkish kids, Moroccan kids. It's a release.

Grime is a group thing. It's music that can be passed down. It needs people. It needs energy. Raw beats, raw lyrics. I think that's what's so key to grime. Everyone can do it. A little kid in Blackpool can start spitting. He's going through exactly the same things that every kid is going through, and he can talk about it. That's how it works. And when he's eighteen he may be doing something. There's another grime kid being born as we speak.

*

We're spitting at 140 miles an hour; you can't always understand how we do it. Like, it's crazy shit and the best MCs are the ones who shout and are craziest. The ones who can go on a stage and go mad, not that but like, if you watch Ghetts perform, so if you watch Crazy Titch perform or you watch someone with energy perform, you'll just be like, 'Fucking hell, they just tore that rave apart.' Do you know what I mean?

As long as you're putting things cleverly, like Jay-Z can still – that Fat Joe remix that he used to do when he was chatting about Beyoncé and shit, obviously he's not chatting about having holes in his zapatos any more or shifting this and shifting that – but you can still say shit about your life in an interesting way, then kids will still want to hear it, I think.

I think that hip hop's different because they don't shout. Like the best rapper is not shouting. The best rappers have got dictionaries beside their beds like bibles. Not necessarily because they need them, but just to enhance what they have: they're very clever and intelligent. The last best rapper, miles ahead of everyone, was Eminem. He had a brain that was miles ahead of everyone, you know what I'm saying? Rappers can do any beat as well. There's 140, maybe 160, you know what I'm saying?

29. Deja Vu

Pirate radio has been a part of anything that's ever come out of England – garage, hardcore, jungle, drum and bass, everything. It was the phone-ins that let me know that it wasn't just a bit of fun. People would ring up and be like, 'Yes, Wiley, you're killing it!' or 'Big up Blah-Blah from Blah-Blah!' and I knew then that we were making a culture.

I've been on pirate radio since I was fourteen. It's the reason I'm Wiley. We were never gonna get a set on Radio 1 or whatever, so we built a fan base ourselves. And it was illegal, you could get arrested and all that, but it was our blessing. You could get charges just for being on a rooftop, but it was our only chance to grasp at. To be honest, it was better than the other stuff we could have been getting up to.

We were always hiding, ducking around, couldn't tell no one where the studio was. It all had to be kept a secret. And it was that element of it that kept it all going. That was part of the magic; because it was illegal, it became a movement.

*

I don't know what would have happened if things went differently that night. It could have been the end. We didn't know how much danger we were in.

This is like summer of 2003. Hot summer. Crazy Titch had just got out of jail, and he'd heard that there was this kid called Dizzee Rascal. Until then, Titch saw himself as the king. But Titch had been away, and now Dizzee was the guy.

So we go to the Deja Vu block in Stratford, in the middle of nowhere, and everybody's there: Roll Deep, Newham Generals, Nasty Crew. That block's gone now, but back then it was mad. I walked out once and this man was waving a shotgun around. Things happened there, you know.

We were in this room, about fifty people, no space, music loud. I was standing next to Dizzee. I spit, then give the mic to Titch. Titch in the middle on a mad ting. Man was sweating, you get me. Titch wanted it. He had this anger and drive that just made him go for it. Plus you've got the fact that one's from Bow, and one's from Stratford. So there's competition. Automatic. So then Titch gives the mic to Dizzee. Dizzee was spitting fire, but not like Titch. Titch was on something else. He takes the mic back, then gives it to Dizzee. So they go back and forth like this, reh reh reh. Energy building. And then suddenly Titch turns to Dizzee, kind of talking at him: 'What?'

Dizzee didn't want to clash, but he just wasn't having it.

Titch pushed Dizzee, and everything just went. Music stopped, Titch bundled through the door onto the rooftop. And then everyone follows. It was a madness. Pitch black. People holding Titch, Dizzee standing shouting, 'Don't hold him back.' Every time we got it calmed, it started up again.

Suddenly I realised that the edge of the roof is right there. No barrier. And I was looking at them, thinking that if Titch breaks through, that would be it. We all could have gone down. Fourteen floors.

It was mad, but that was the scene back then.

30. Mention My Name

Janaya

Kylea's career taking off wasn't always a good thing. Some of the stuff from those early days on pirate radio were ridiculous.

When I was in Year 9, I was going out for lunch and got cornered on the pavement by these boys from Stratford who knew who I was. They took my phone and rang Kylea up and said, 'We've got your sister and we want £40,000.' He just went, 'Keep her,' and hung up.

He was on the radio at that time, I recorded the session – all you can hear is him saying, '£40,000? You what? Keep her.' I was really scared. And then I remember he paged me and said, 'Whatever you do, just act like I don't really care. They'll let you go, because I'm not giving no money. They're not even serious. Trust me, I know what I'm doing.'

These boys were saying, 'Your brother's so out of order – he said to keep you.' So I was like, 'OK, so now what?' I was thinking, 'I'm gonna get killed or something.' Then I realised I knew one of them – a friend's cousin – and she'd come round and gone, 'What are you doing?! That's my best friend!' So they let me go.

He would say, 'Just don't worry about it. I'm making money for us.' But I was getting the backlash.

*

I remember when I was fourteen, all the kids at my school would listen to Rinse on a Sunday and talk about it the next day: 'Oh my god, did you hear this clash, did you hear this, did you hear that? Did you hear your brother's set?'

At that time Bashy was my favourite MC. I would go round telling anyone who would listen, 'Bashy's the hardest! He's the best!' I'd never met him before, but I was practically screaming his name from the rooftops.

One Monday I came into school, and there was this really weird vibe. Then someone took me aside and asked if I'd heard the clash with Bashy and my brother at the weekend. I had no idea what they were on about. So then they were like, 'Bashy said your name during the set – he said to Wiley, "I fucked your sister in the street."'

I was heartbroken. I knew it was a bag of rubbish, but I was still so upset. Kylea was like, 'What are you upset for? You know it's not the truth,' but I was angry because I'd gone around singing his praises. And I was so young! At that age I wanted to be a journalist, to work for a radio station, and this totally shattered my confidence. I didn't want to be involved in this kind of thing. It was evil to me. Once you put something out there about someone, it's too late to correct it.

Then one night, Flow Dan's girlfriend had a party. I ended up running into Bashy in the corridor. I stared him dead in the eye and said, 'You all right?' It was like he looked right through me. I said, 'It's Janaya,' and he was like, 'Who's Janaya?'

I reminded him of the things he said about me on the radio, and finally the penny dropped. He was so apologetic, trying to explain himself to me – like, 'Oh, you know what it's like, you just want to clash the best.' He said, 'Nothing can ever get to your brother. He's so great that anything you say to him just goes over his head, and this is the way I knew I could properly wind him up. I was trying to win.'

I left it with him on all right terms, said that we're cool. But years later at the Radio 1 Weekender in Leeds, I was with Skepta looking for the bar and bumped into Bashy. He asked if he could come with us, and Skepta just brushed him off and said, 'Janaya, let's go.' He properly stuck up for me. He had my back.

31. Word of Mouth

Richard Senior

I used to run around with Kylea and Logan, we used to drive around meeting people. There were a lot of different artists popping up all over the place. That was the first time I met Lethal B, in Chingford. Then you had people like Ghetts, Dizzee, Kano, Nasty Crew. And Rhythm Division on Roman Road was where it all happened. They'd all get together there and spit, battling on the mic.

I remember the first time I heard Kylea clash. For some reason I was sitting in the van with Danny Weed just outside our flat. We were supposed to be somewhere, but we couldn't move. It was Wiley and Durrty Doogz. I had to listen to the whole set. That was pirate radio. It had me. It just kept me hooked, you know, not only what was being said, but also the energy that was put into it. Just listening to these guys battling each other. And that started with Wiley. He introduced an element of competition.

So after that I would listen whenever they were on the radio. Rinse FM or wherever. When they were on, I'd tune in.

I also got to hang out with him in the studio occasionally. I was there when he made 'Ground Zero', for example. That was a very, very close song for me, you know. Because the Twin Towers had just gone down, and we had family in America. At first we didn't know whether anyone we knew was inside when they collapsed. I remember watching footage on the television, and just thinking it was so unreal. We didn't know what to think, or what to say. But Wiley made this song that day that kind of expressed what we were feeling in some way.

32. Lyrical Exercise

'*Tiger, see me affi creep up on the riddim like a spider,*
Nuff a dem ah my yout, nuff a dem ah minor ...'

Wretch 32

Back in the day, I was just hungry. I was listening to
what was going on underground, listening to the radio,
trying to hear who the new MCs were. There was a
swing from garage to something new, it was almost like
a new genre had been created, and Wiley was at the
forefront of that. So there was garage. And out of garage
came this new thing. Something with a little vibe. We
didn't know what it was, but it was creative, and it was
fresh, and it was innovative.

I've always been a writer, and I've always been a
creator myself. I was spitting on any instrumentals I
could get my hands on. I was spitting over reggae, I was
spitting over R. Kelly. It was whatever I had to hand.
If any artist left a spare eight bars, I'd loop those eight
bars to a sixty-four and make a song. I'd make a song
out of anything – Michael Jackson, you name it.

The pirate radio thing was happening. Everyone was
going on for two hours or so. Everyone spitting over
instrumentals, most of which Wiley had created. By that

time, my head was in song format. Radio was part of creating, part of the process. I was sharpening my skills on the airwaves and going along with that.

When I got to know him I was in a crew called the Movement. And he was in Boy Better Know. The journalists kind of got into this thing that there was something going on with Boy Better Know and the Movement, slyly. Fans picked it up. And people would see us on the street and say, 'You know what, I prefer Boy Better Know' or 'I prefer the Movement.' We felt the pressure to get into a little bit of lyrical exercise, which probably didn't need to happen, but it did. It's part of all our journeys, and we have to accept that.

I try not to clash with anyone. I try to compete through my songs, through doing collaborations with other artists. If I feel like someone's big, I'll try and do a song with them. We'll see who has the best verse when we're all on a song together. I don't want to feel like I'm waking up focusing my energy on someone else. In a negative format. I've had top ten records about my two children. That's inspiring for me. That's inspiring for them. I don't know who I'm going to inspire writing a diss song.

Sometimes there's pressure, because someone says this, someone says that. But everything you say on those songs, you have to live with, and your family has to live with. It's one of those things. Everyone's in their own lane. If you're into that, you're into that.

33. No Rules

Logan Sama

Wiley had been an influence on me before I ever met
him. I was out in Essex at that time; I was in my late
teens, so everything I was hearing was off Deja Vu or
Sidewinder tape packs. I'd bought 'Nicole's Groove', and
then he started making tunes like 'Terrible' and 'Know
We', so I was buying all the iterations I could get my
hands on. He stood out, for me, because of that skippy
flow – it wasn't really like anything else I'd heard. It was
distinctive.

In 2002 I got onto Rinse FM, on a 7 p.m. Friday-night
slot. And when I got there for my first ever show, Pay
As U Go were being interviewed by the *Observer* in the
studio – a big, derelict community centre in Dagenham
Heathway. I wasn't shy about talking to them. If
someone creates something that brings me happiness,
I don't feel a kind of way about letting them know. So it
was cool for me to be able to meet them in person, and
show them love. To appreciate the people responsible for
creating something that I enjoy. I wanted to let Wiley
know that he'd reached me, outside of his immediate
circle of influence. You're in a council estate in east
London, I'm in Brentwood and I'm a massive fan of what
you do.

Roll Deep had the 9 p.m. slot after me, and I didn't want to risk losing signal on the drive back home to Essex. So I'd stay and listen. Wiley, Danny Weed, Flow Dan and Dizzee Rascal were putting out this crazy, experimental music. You couldn't hear it anywhere else. It was an absolute joy to be able to sit in and hear tracks literally come from the studio to the cutting house to be played on the radio for the first time. Wiley was an inspiration to all of us. He gave a voice to kids from council estates for the first time. And in their own voice too. Not in an American accent, or using American slang. People looked up to him – especially people from Bow, and especially Dizzee.

There was a logical progression from garage. 'Nicole's Groove' is obviously a garage record, and Pay As U Go were channelling a lot of that dark, underground garage sound. The change came as the sound became more dub-orientated, with people coming over from jungle and drum and bass and bringing their perspective with them. When I got into garage it was a very diverse sound, but round about the millennium it became really homogenised and saccharine, a lot more commercial. It didn't excite me any more. But on pirate radio and in the clubs they were making music with no rules.

A lot of the business practices in the early days of grime were influenced by the roads. You'd go to the pressing plant, pick up your boxes of records, go out and drive around, sell them at a profit, and then at the end of the day you take home your profit and re-up tomorrow. It's just like shotting. That's why grime's always had an entrepreneurial spirit, because it was necessary – the garage scene had disassociated itself from the underground, the crews and the MCing. There were UK garage committees that were purposefully trying to blacklist artists. They wanted to separate themselves out from a council estate scene they considered uneducated, aggy, rough. Back in 2001, 2002, people didn't understand the culture. We were coming off the back of Ali G, where MCing is seen as a big joke; it wasn't being respected as an art form. Everyone looked down on the kids in tracksuits, talking in a language they didn't really understand. So the artists making music out of their bedrooms had no one to help them with the business side. It had to be all DIY.

We started out with white labels and tapes, moved on to CDs and MP3s, and now streaming is the biggest thing for us. It was the first genre in this country to be born with the Internet, to be spread virally. We had the tape packs, the raves and the club nights, but it really exploded when we started file sharing. We were swapping stuff on MSN Messenger all the time, and young producers were using whatever technology they had around them. So Wiley was using the Korg Triton for his signature bass sounds, but most kids were using cracked software. It was more of that illicit pirate spirit – get it done, any way you can. Grime is an ever-evolving organism that adapts to its surroundings. That's why it's survived this long.

Those early days of grime were very rough around the edges. It was exactly as the lyrics portrayed. So you'd be going to EQ's in Stratford and having to go through metal detectors, and all the local gangs would be in there alongside music lovers. Inner-city London was listening to grime, and inner-city London was out raving to grime. But a lot of the time the issues that came up were because of artists having problems with each other. I know Wiley suffered because of that.

34. Confidence

'Me and Dizzee made it an occupation.'
Speakerbox

When I first met Dizzee I wasn't Wiley. I wasn't there yet. It was only when I made *Step 1–20* that I became Wiley, you know? I'd done some freestyles before, but with that, I sprayed my heart out to high heaven. It's not that anyone even cared about it really, but I just felt that I knew what I was capable of. I'd killed it in there as much as I could. So after that, I said, 'Yeah, I'm Wiley. I know I'm Wiley because if you give me a three-minute, four-minute beat I can write to the end of it and I can spit bars. I'm Wiley.' But when I met Dizzee I wasn't Wiley yet. I wasn't good yet. I was still listening to garage, and still new to MCing.

We were together all the time, all the time. Like, Dizzee used to get a cab to our house in the mornings and get me up. Sometimes I am a bit lazy. He was like, 'Nah, man, we've gotta be great, we don't just wanna be good, we've gotta be great.' He'd get me up, and we'd go. To the studio, to an event, to the radio.

Dizzee was young, he was energetic, he used to do a lotta dirty stuff which is why his first album was probably a reflection of that. He was very determined to win. To get there. Do you know why? Because he knew how good he was already. I wasn't there, and I don't think many of us were, really. But he was. If we were invited onto the radio back then we'd be a little nervous, talking about what to play and what might happen. Not knowing ourselves. He already knew: 'I'm going on the radio and I'm gonna spray and everyone's gonna be talking about me after because I am the kid.' No question. He knew that. He never said it, because he didn't have to say it. He was very confident. He knew how much better than everyone he was and that's why I've always had respect for him.

35. Pay As U Go

When south London heard Pay As U Go for the first time, they knew the jig was up.

Pay As U Go was like a crew of headliners. Each person was important, and had their own special skill. You had people who were DJing, someone who was great at clashing, someone who was good at the radio and dah di-dah di-dah di-dah. Every individual could hold down a set on their own, could probably have made it on their own. It was like a supergroup.

You've got to remember that So Solid were like the maddest, baddest thing at that time. They had the flash cars, the girls, the fame – like they were on *Top of the Pops*! Like Asher D, Lisa Maffia, Romeo and Oxide & Neutrino all popping off. And Megaman was at the top of it all.

Mega was the architect of the whole thing. And he made sure that nobody fucked with a single member of the crew. This was when you had Tottenham dons living in south London: walking around and going swimming at Streatham Baths like nothing. So Solid had the backing of some real people. Don't get confused. They might have been rolling around in Porsches and getting bigged up by Jamie Theakston and whatever, but they were on some road shit.

I used to go round south a lot, to get vinyl from Red Records in Brixton. So I was known around there from early. Everyone expected Dizzee to get absolutely seen off in that Westwood clash with Asher D, but he didn't. Imagine seeing So Solid with all that fame, all that money, and then these bruk-pocket half-yardie geezers from east turn up with an even colder sound.

With Pay As U Go there was a lot of memories there. Not dramas, but we were learning a lot, in Pay As U Go. Everyone was like their own person, their own character. It was like – how can I say it? – I reckon, without those years none of us would even be here either, like I think them years, the arguments, the deals, the record deals, the turning left, right, the fact that I was going to be roading anyway, and the fact that Paco and Plague are the ones who even started Pay As U Go with Slimzee.

I think they were stepping stones. Because I hate to look at it as a stepping stone because obviously it's a powerful part, but like it's something, it's not a minor, but it's one of the stepping stones. Led to me meeting Dizzee Rascal, whatever like, you know, like meeting Nick Denton, the manager, meeting other people who make music as well.

There was no champs, no profiling, no beautiful people. Just us raggo East End lads in trackies and hoods, hanging out in some shithole white-man pub on

Old Kent Road. We were realer in a way. We were just about spitting and making beats, that's it. All the majors were signing pop and 2-step, and we were coming out with a grimey Eski sound. South must have thought we were on some Crackney shit.

'Champagne Dance' was everywhere in 2001, from the roads to the raves. And my verse made me an icon.

36. Rolling Deep

Scratchy

I've been doing music since for ever. For me it begins
with garage. It was those MCs that inspired us – there
were less vocals on the track, so there was space for us
to do our little thing. It was just us kids from around
the area really. We started out just mimicking what we
heard on the radio. I'd be doing Creed and PSG's voices,
spitting their lyrics as a way of getting into the music.
It's how I learnt to match a beat, to stay in time.

I didn't actually meet Wiley through music. We met
on the football pitch. Bartlett Park. I was thirteen, the
youngest on the team, so I didn't really have a position.
I just ran where people told me. He was on the other
team, I remember him being actually really good!
Wiley's five years older than me, which now is nothing,
but then it felt like miles between us.

I'd bunk off school a lot, so when I did actually turn
up, everyone thought I was a new kid. It's not cos I was
bad or anything, I was just shy. I think that's why I
was drawn to DJing. There's decks between you and
everyone else. I didn't want to go to school: I just wanted
to go up to my bedroom and mix, put the headphones
over my ears and go into my own world.

I started doing radio stations, like Flava FM and that. This was when I was about fifteen. Wiley was on Rinse, but I had a show with his cousin Biggie Pitbull. I was his DJ and we had started getting pretty good, and we were around the right people – Nasty Crew had just started. So we'd got his attention, and one day he rung me up and asked if I wanted to join Roll Deep. That's the first time I really knew that I was sick at what I do.

That was an amazing phone call. It was like getting an upgrade. Me and Biggie went over to Rinse, which caused a bit of upset with the rest of our crew. I guess Wiley thought we were just better. To this day some of Flying Squad will say, 'You should have stayed with us, we could have made it happen!' and I'll be like, 'Sure ...'

Pay As U Go came first, so obviously I'd heard 'Champagne Dance' and 'Know We' and all that. I'd seen the video, I'd seen them get big. I looked up to them, but I wasn't actually aware of the fame and the chart positions, the money that was there to be made. I was just into the music. At some point Wiley and Flow Dan decided to move away from all that and start Roll Deep. They wanted to make their own crew.

It was a real DIY vibe with Roll Deep. Flow Dan and Wiley would come up to my bedroom, when I was bunking off school, and just start rapping over the beats I played for them. It was all vinyl, like garage instrumentals. White labels. We'd record tapes and listen back to them, hear how good we were getting.

That was the original start, the two of them in my room when I should have been in class.

The rapport was incredible. It was inspirational to be around. I watched what they were doing so closely – their patterns, their flow, their mic control – and it made me want to do it too. So I'd write a little lyric. I'd say a little bar. I used to be scared of MCing, I was like, 'Oh, how are people gonna take me?' Then I got my confidence because of seeing those two come up. I found my own voice.

It wasn't as easy to become an MC back then – we didn't have SoundCloud, we had to work hard to find the records, and there wasn't anyone to listen to us. It's not like today, where someone retweets something and suddenly you're working with OVO. We had to graft. We'd be up in my room for hours and hours with the decks, just looking for a song that was good enough to put lyrics over. We didn't care about the money then – maybe you lose a bit of the passion when the paycheques start coming in. It becomes a job.

Wiley was that person who'd get me in the studio, either with him or booking me my own time. He brought me out of myself really – my dad had just passed away, and I was sort of floating around, dragging my feet, hitting the top of a wall with a stick. I was at that age where if I didn't have the music, or the right people around me, I would have been in jail. I would have done something stupid. Wiley was like a brother to me. When I was struggling with rent he'd say, 'Don't worry, Scratch, I got this.'

37. Lucid

Richard Senior

It was like a sport for them. And like with any sport, the more you practised the better you got. You'd know, going on pirate radio stations wasn't easy. You didn't know what was going to happen. But if you had practised, you were prepared.

Battling's hard. If you're clashing, then you can't make stuff up. You have to know what you're talking about. If you don't, you lose your credibility. It's when the battle starts to move away from the mic to the streets that it becomes dangerous. But battle bars are not designed to be pleasant. It's not new. Punk is an aggressive music, for example. They weren't saying nice things. It was kind of a reaction to the music of the time, maybe.

Nobody in this music is in a perfect situation, you know, otherwise it wouldn't be called grime. Why did this music come about? Anger, aggression, frustration – at life in general, at people, at mums and dads. At maybe not having a perfect life.

'Ice Rink', 'Eskimo', that was the coldness of surviving, that was the coldness of life, the coldness of being rushed, and run down, and having to fend for yourself. It came from his struggle as a young person to make it. To have his own thing. To have money. And yeah, he had personal stuff going on. Myself and his mum not being together, that kind of stuff. His mum and I would speak, and she always encouraged me to be there for him. And I was there.

But I was also working a lot when he was growing up. I never really knew what to expect when I came home. I used to work shifts, so I could be at home at any time, and out at any time. Night, day, even a couple of days. Once you started a job, you finished it. If I was working nights, I'd come back and sleep. It could all be quiet, with Kylea just working on the computer, or there could be thirty people spitting with someone holding an aerial out of the window. He used to steal my van to go raving. I would go to sleep and the van was there, wake up and it was gone.

We also got arrested. One day there was a knock on the door, and it was the police. They had come round about something that had happened on the street. I don't really know what went on, but they wanted to search the house. We weren't resisting arrest as such, but we were making a verbal demonstration. And so they arrested both of us.

I gave my parents the same. I'd disappear and not come back for a minute, or go raving and stay out. Just doing what teenagers do. What goes around comes around, I suppose. There was a little bit of tension, we had our disagreements, and he decided, 'Well, look, I'm going to do my thing.'

*

He's got his reasons for not turning up to certain things. Grime at times was a dangerous platform. You could go to the radio, and come out, and there would be someone sitting there waiting for you. You could say something about someone and that person hasn't taken it the way you meant, and before you know it there's the road beef that you have to deal with. It's not everywhere you can go. I knew that then. So if he didn't turn up, in my head I knew why. It was dangerous, for sure. People have lost their lives in this business. People have gone through some heavy shit in this business. If I'm going to come, or it's just me and a friend walking into an arena, I don't know who is looking at me, or who's going to run out, or who's going to protect me. It's not always easy.

He's older now. I don't see the danger that I saw back then. Going to his concerts now, I'm proud and grateful to the most high, that he got to actually get to that situation, where he could look around at people who probably didn't mean him that well back in the day, but they're there now, and everyone's calm, and everyone's cool, because everyone's a little bit older now, so that kind of battling bullshit from back in the day is all gone.

I was scared for him. From the time that the clashing started, and the clashing began to slip out onto the road. People would spit bars and say what they're going to do. It was a bit like a verbal Twitter. Except that you heard it in a bar.

The thing about it was that I couldn't be with him all the time. I definitely couldn't advise him on what he should do all the time. I think if I did that he wouldn't be who he is now. He had to fight through to get to where he was going. Which he did. Apart from the music, the tenacity of his spirit, to stick with this, throughout all of that? You've got to commend him for that. He's my son. I love him, and I love what he's done. He took my dreams to the next level.

38. The Getalong Gang

'It looks all good from the outside
Creps and cars and bikes and sleepless nights
And pointless fights in the manor.
Everybody wants to be top boy in the manor.'
Doorway

In the world of man running out and spraying bars, no one ain't chatting to us. They're not. Americans are not. They're rapping. They're chatting to us if they're in the booth, in their car. They're not chatting to us on a stage, running out. Only ragga man are. And that's where we got it from in the first place.

I never clashed for nothing. I used to clash for reasons. Clashing was a test. Say we're on the radio, and someone comes in, for example. They have a bar for me, so I have a bar for them.

No one from my day wants to battle any more. I suppose to still be battling after twenty years says something as well. Maybe no one really respects you if you've never moved on. I'd still do it, but that's just how crazy I am. It's good to keep the battle chip in your body. We pick at the silliest things when we clash. You can lose a battle just because the other person's got a hundred grand, and you've only got a fiver. 'Oh, you're shit because you haven't got Louis Vuittons on.' That's got nothing to do with how good you are!

The first battle I lost in my spirit was against Durrty Doogz and Commander B, in the Eskimo Dance. I had nowhere to run. And then there was the Movement ting. At first, it was just me against Ghetts. And then all of a sudden it was me against the Movement. But I still went forward. I listened to them, and I was like, 'Shit, man. It's me against five, six, seven MCs. I need to do some shit that keeps me existing past this, because it's getting dangerous. There's no one on my side wanting to back me.' I made it through, just about.

Durrty Doogz is my lyrical nemesis. Which is why we reunited and dropped that EP. It was about taking it back to when we were spitting bars and just trying to be better than each other. Only now I'm not trying to take off his head and he's not trying to take off my head.

The person I don't actually talk to, out of everyone I've ever had lyrical confrontation with, would probably be Trim. Not that I don't want to, but we're on different paths. We had our little thing back in 2009, 2010, war dubs and that: 'For whatever reason, I'm big in Billericay.' It comes from the fact that two people with two fiery temperaments in one crew will never work. Ever.

Sometimes in the same crew you battle for fun. But when me and him battle, it's poison. Because he's a dark yout. When me and him war, we're not just saying, 'You're a dickhead.' There's some real things being said.

I've had clashes with everyone, you know. I even had a little ting with Skepta at Red Bull. He was clashing, we had our team lined up, and then Tempa T walked out. We're both thinking, 'What's Tempa T doing here?' So I tried to speak to him, to tell him to relax. And he turns round and says, 'Shush!' At the time, I didn't register it, but later that evening, watching the footage, I thought, 'He just told me to shush on the big stage!'

I wasn't happy, but I was cool. If he was around me, I was cool. Do you know what I mean? I wasn't going to go to his yard and drag him out.

When I walk out my house to clash, I forget that I've got a mum and dad and sisters and family. I don't want to drag them into it. I know that it's just about me, and the person. When I'm talking, I'm talking to the person, about the person, only. Mostly.

There's a rudeboy thing, which we get from dancehall, so you might throw a little 'Your mum' in there. But it's not that important, some people do tolerate that and some people don't tolerate that. I go to war, no family. I go to war, knowing my ability and anticipating what to say.

When you go to war, it's about lies, truth and rumour. Remember that: every war is just lies, truth and rumour.

If you hear something about someone, and you go to a war and say it and it's not true, it just slides off. It's just a rumour. But if you know something about someone, it's not a rumour: it's a jab. It'll hit them properly.

I've had so many clashes and I've enjoyed them all. It doesn't matter what's happened in the clash. I've walked out, I've carried on, I've gone to the studio, I've kept working. No one's been able to end me, because I haven't let them. No MC could ever make me stop.

Clashing is a cussing match on a beat, but it's also a sport just like boxing. I know what I've won, and I know what I've lost. Twitter isn't clashing. On Twitter, I'm just running psyches. It's not even a bad-mind ting. Man run psyches on man. We're not going to fight or nothing.

The clash with Kano was a big one. I've got a lot of respect for Kano. Kano is a clever man. A lot cleverer than people think. That's all I can say. People don't actually know how clever he is. He went through some shit when he grew up, but he made it out. I never realised it at the time. Life was so mad back then.

That day I went to Jammer's house, to work in the studio, but all of a sudden it was like, 'No! You're gonna clash Kano today!'

I was like, 'Whoa, I don't really wanna clash Kano today,' but I couldn't say no. They knew that I didn't wanna clash Kano, but I had to take the battle. I couldn't back down. I wish I did, though.

Imagine! You're going along minding your own business, then someone comes along and says you have to clash this kid. I thought he was sick! If you were Wiley, and you walked into someone's house and they said you had to clash Kano, or you had to clash Dizzee, and you knew how good they are – would you have done it? I know a couple man who would have just let it go. I was set up.

He was seventeen years old, fresh and clear. I was a bit older, not as fluent as him. But if I had gone there and been ready, it might have been a whole different outcome.

In that clash, Kano thought he was Tyson. Thing is, I'm not Tyson either. But after that clash I went on a Tyson tirade. After I lost I went and won about ten more, and Kano never battled again. That let me know that he weren't a savage – he's the good boy, and *I'm* the savage. No disrespect to Kano, cos he's great. But he's clean-cut. He can paint a good picture, but he's not Van Gogh.

Gangsters

I been away for a year, have sway for a year
Here's a few new stars, I've got two new cars, I'm with
   (Gangsters)
I went from dough to broke. How'd I survive? Because I
   think like (Gangsters)
Come with me to HMP and I'll show you (Gangsters)
Aright, God, I see you put me with the (Gangsters)
I know your crew stacks, blud, you and your boys could
   never be (Gangsters)
I don't mean TV, blud, I mean real life (Gangsters)
I got a Turkish bredrin from school, we're cool, his family are
   (Gangsters)
Listen, Fire Camp, you ain't (Gangsters)
They say how can you make a fortune if you are
   (Gangsters)?
That's easy, shot the peng through from here to North
   Weezy (Gangsters)

I was in Ministry, look over there. Yeah, I can see them
    (Gangsters)
Scored your wifey and she had dampers
West End, I was with (Gangsters)
We just had a wave of new (Gangsters)
Yeah, I think there's been a rise, more (Gangsters)
Imagine that, I'm a street kid, brainy like (Gangsters)
Nick and Dyl can relate, watch (Gangsters)
Like I don't know Vinyl Star and all the old-time Brixton
    (Gangsters)
When I was a kid, south-west 28s, letting off twenty-eight
    like (Gangsters)
Me and D-Roll know you were squeezing hard, you're one of
    them (Gangsters)
I've never ever seen you with no (Gangsters)
They'll teach you a lesson, don't mess with (Gangsters)
I go all around the world and meet (Gangsters)
They know my name, why? Cos I hustle in the music game
    with (Gangsters)
God's Gift from Skepta, know what I'm saying?
The government tried to destroy my race but them man
    turned into (Gangsters)
You think when Yanks come to England, they want to be
    around them (Gangsters)?
I don't think so, whole security firm on the scene
Got the red beam on the biggest man in your team, they'll
    crumble your dreams
Listen up, they're (Gangsters)
I warn the kids, once you get dark, you turn to (Gangsters)

Feel the dark force, police are scared, true stories
(Gangsters)
When they leave the scene, the whole scene looks gory
(Gangsters)
Let me call Picky, it's getting a bit sticky, I know them
(Gangsters)
I know Billy and Boogie, they always tell me, 'Control your
(Gangsters)'
I'm in Sidewinder, look around, I see a few (Gangsters)
Not many, but the ones I'm with – they're heavy, ready
(Gangsters)
When the shells start spraying (Gangsters)
I got stabbed fourteen times, I can tell you it weren't by
(Gangsters)
My uncle got stabbed like twice and he died, I tell you, he's
one of them (Gangsters)
I was in Nottingham, who showed me love? A whole crew of
(Gangsters)
On the road, it's not a joke, you don't want beef with
(Gangsters)
Mega and Dizzee, the beef weren't small, some different
(Gangsters)
Back to England and squash the beef, leave that on the
island, dead that (Gangsters)
That's what it's like when you're with (Gangsters)
That's what it's like when you're with (Gangsters)
Eskiboy, I roll with (Gangsters)
You can't stop me, I'm with (Gangsters)
Roll Deep, we are (Gangsters)

East side, we are (Gangsters)
North-west, we are (Gangsters)
South-west, we are (Gangsters)
South-east, we are (Gangsters)
Up north, we are (Gangsters)

39. Blackwall

I didn't see his face.

We had left Bow. Me and Target were in the car, about to approach the Blackwall Tunnel. I was in beef. I used to sell weed at this time, I was carrying things at this time, because you never know – and I realised that one guy on a moped had been following us for ages. I was looking in the rear-view thinking: 'Shit, who is this?' He was wearing a luminous jacket and a helmet. He pulled up slowly – so slowly that I got the time to think: 'Right, he's coming to shoot me.' I mean, he probably was.

So I panicked. The traffic slowed down so I opened the door of the car, more because I didn't want to get shot through the window. But as I swung the door he panicked too, and swerved on the bike – imagining that I was gonna pull something, I guess. He sped past but we were just stuck there. The cars weren't moving, just bibbing their horns. Everything stopped.

I didn't see where he went. Suddenly the cars started moving again. Rather than go straight on we drove over the pavement and turned back on ourselves. I thought we were good, but I looked behind and the bike was still following us. Can you believe it? We managed to lose him eventually, but it was not good.

Later on I found out who the guy was. I'd never say though. It's not important. That was the first time I realised that this is just how it goes. If you want to be out there, to play that game, this is a part of it. You're never going to be safe. That's just how it is.

Kylea Part 2

Richard Senior and Janaya Cowie

Janaya: He went to Homerton Hospital that time. Remember?

Richard Senior: Yeah, yeah. But where was that hospital we went ...? White City, Shepherd's Bush, yeah. That was a bad one. The place was like overrun, it took the whole place over. People were coming from everywhere, journalists, cameras and all this and all that, and there were all kind of people there. And there was no privacy. There was no privacy.

J: They told us he was going to be OK, so we weren't too worried about him by that point, but the number of people there was getting tiresome. We didn't know who they all were.

R: The violence has always been there.

J: It's associated with the culture, isn't it. It's the same in America, people think rap and hip hop are somehow connected to gangs, to drugs and gun crime. Some people may have come from those backgrounds, but a lot didn't. It doesn't define the music.

R: No, but it's a part of it. I remember going to a show with him, and on the way he got a phone call, and the person said, 'I wouldn't bother coming down here,' and Kylea was like, 'What? Look yeah, what's happening?' And whoever it was said, 'Because so-and-so's here,' warning him that there was going to be trouble.

J: That happened a lot. But he would always get a call first, if it looked dangerous or there were people there that he didn't get on with.

R: The thing is, the roads and the music kind of go hand in hand in the sense that a lot of the people that are in the music started on the road. But it also works the other way round.

J: Things can get serious quite quickly. When him and Ghetts had their little thing, I was the one trying to sort it all out. I was the one in bed with two phones, talking to people and switching the phones over, and just trying to calm things down really. My ears were red.

R: I met Ghetts again probably about a few years after and I said, 'Listen, the last time I saw you, it was hotting up.' He said, 'Yeah I know, that was back then, wasn't it.' So in other words, most of the people that he's ever had any trouble with have always come back. They've grown up.

J: I love Ghetts to bits, you know. In fact, I can't honestly say there's anyone from that time that I haven't got any respect for. The ones that are actually, that have done it, that have got through, all right, yeah, they may have said things, nasty things, about family and stuff like that …

R: Yes, they did. But they're only words, you know, and that's the nature of that genre, that music.

J: I remember Kylea used to always give me loads of money. I was like: 'Right, thanks, but my life is ruined, because of what's being said. And you're just sitting in the house, worrying about your own stuff.' It was just like a playground. Imagine a bad boys' playground, just boys cussing each other. Because that's what boys do. Have cussing matches. And I was like, nah.

R: But it was just the music.

J: Yeah. I used to get really upset, then I'd think to myself: 'Do you know like, it's not worth taking too seriously. It is what it is.'

R: Exactly.

J: They were doing it to win. And I'm like, 'Yeah I know, but that kind of ruined my school life.'

40. Pinches

'If you do wrong then you get paid back. We call it pay back.'
Goin' Mad

You can't come to my door and rob me. I'm the same as the people on the street, but I'm not.

I have grown though. If someone does something wrong, you might want to respond. But when you get older, you can't always fight back. You've got shit to lose. That's where I made my mistakes. Always fighting back. But the people I was fighting were not in my position. They can do certain things, and you can't.

The thing is when you associate yourself with knives and guns, you become a part of something you can't escape from. The person who murdered my uncle got stabbed and killed; the person who slashed me across the face died recently too. What goes around comes around. There's consequences to everything you do. What can I say? If you live that way, you'll die that way.

Even the most evil guy is street famous. In my school, all my mates used to love the Krays. But if you knew what they actually did, would you still love them? There was this one man from the ends who used to show up at the local swimming pool. As soon as he turned up, everyone left the pool. Man was just chilling doing breast stroke on his own. But that was a kind of fame. People feared him, but people loved him. Some of these guys were heroes as well, not just out on the street doing this or that. They were like superheroes.

The difference between my day and now is that everyone knew who was bad, cos everyone would talk about it. You can't win any more. Now it doesn't matter what colour you are – he's black, he's white, he's Turkish – anyone can be a rudeboy. That's the danger, that anyone can be bad. It could be a kid that everyone was bullying who then turns around and switches. People are quicker to turn around and say, 'Nah, that's not happening.'

I'm from east London, I'm from Bow. But I was never just in Bow. I went all around. Wherever you had a cousin, or a mate, or family, you go there, you check them. So I was in every part of London while I was growing up.

I was always aware of violence, and it wasn't just black-on-black. How can people get hold of guns in London? Who controls the underworld? None of these black boys. Black boys don't control the underworld that created twenty-five, thirty-odd years of black-on-black violence. Just the smaller stuff – looking at each other wrong, stepping on each other's feet, drug dealing. There were a lot of people falling out. There was a lot of robbing. A lot of kidnapping, stabbing, shooting. One time I went to this jungle rave, and I could see some kind of fracas – I don't know who was beefing who – up on the balcony. And all of a sudden, someone threw someone else over the balcony.

But I'm not surprised. Think about it. Years and years ago, in the days of sword and shield, it was much worse than it is now. Arms chopped off, do you know what I'm saying? It's just the history of men and violence. So knife crime doesn't shock me. I'm not surprised at all – and if you are, you're just acting like King Richard and all these other guys never had a sword, do you know what I mean?

In Bow people talk. If someone's gonna do something to you, you'll hear people chatting shit before anything happens.

I've got a kind of hazard perception, so that if anyone truly dark ever kicked near me, I'd have to move. Because there's some evil shit that goes on – I've had dark hours up to my eyeballs. I've been rushed, I've been beaten up, I've been stabbed. I've seen people kept hostage. So I have this threshold now: something in me can see, can feel, when something is beyond the normal run of beef and dramas.

The dark hours made me get older. I thought I was bad; like something would happen and I'd go out carrying, out for revenge. And absolutely nothing would happen. Then when I didn't carry anything, that's when I'd go out and get run down, get chased. It's karma, this kind of stuff, and it's dangerous.

*

I know what a knife is.

It all started with me because of a friend of mine. That's always the way – if you don't start something yourself, you get dragged into someone else's situation. So that's what happened with this. My friend. Someone owed him money, but wasn't paying. He saw the person, he dealt with the situation. But the person who owed him money had a cousin. They remembered what happened.

Two days later I went to do a rave. I was with my guy. We were about two metres from the stage when all of a sudden I see like this person running towards me. Then another, then another. Like twenty-five kids jump over. It happens. I got stabbed seven times. In my side, in my arm, in my bum, in the back of my leg. They had to put a tube in my side to drain the blood or whatever.

I came out of hospital like two weeks, two and a half weeks later. This is an east London ting. So I go shopping in west London to buy some trainers, and I walk into Global Sports, and the boy who stabbed me is walking out. So I hit him. I wasn't even thinking. But he was with two people. They stabbed me six, seven times again. But this time they had like a small knife, a Stanley knife. All I could feel was pinches.

I almost died. They took me to hospital and I tried to get out: 'I need to go home!' And they said, 'Sit down.' Stayed in hospital for a while.

I got out eventually, built up my strength, went out to a rave and saw the same boy again! But this time I didn't do anything.

41. Unstoppable

Logan Sama

The first time I met Jammer was when we had to go and see Wiley in hospital. This was just after he'd been stabbed several times at a club. We go there and he was walking around his room, in a gown, with a tube coming out of his side draining his lung into a bucket. It was serious. But he was absolutely adamant that he wasn't going to let the people that had done this stop him. He had all his stitches in, he'd been stabbed a lot, and he had a punctured lung. He checked himself out that day, and went and MCed at Eskimo Dance the next night. He is impossible to stop.

42. Crazy Titch

I just want man to be free. If he hadn't gone to jail, Crazy Titch would've blown up. He would have been massive. He was the rudeboy MC – shouting, jumping around, badding up all the MCs there – he was the king of that sort of thing.

Titch should not be where he is. He should not be in jail for thirty years, but he made a decision to defend his older brother. I'm not hating on that situation, it was a decision that any brother of his blood would make.

I realised something. If I've got a brother, and he's going through something, I have to help him. I have to help him unconditionally. Especially if we're quite close.

If your brother calls you and asks for help, then you've got to go. You might run into all kinds of trouble, but you've got to go.

You jump. If your brother's in trouble, then you jump.

I believe that if Crazy Titch had not jumped, he would be the king. He would be the one all the kids looked up to, the role model.

Stormy Weather

That's why we're the best, have a conflict
Then we go and do somethin' fresh
Don't get test with levels are way higher
I shoot for the target, call me Aim Higher
Merk guys on the mic and up the high life
Wiley, Wiley, you're on a high
Shut your mouth, blud, I was born on a high
See, you don't know this could be your last night
I'm passed right, I'm on another level you can't see
That's why you can't dark me, join the nasty
Won't work, end here, I'm worth two dubs, none of the marvy
I'm hardly touched, I got an army though
They'll rain on – how'd you think you got your chain on?
You shit bricks when I bring the pain on
Better switch your brain on, you can see I'm way gone
Look back, the game's gone, you got caught up in
Stormy weather

That's why I'm a grafter, the tag-team master
Don't know now, you will realise after
I've made my mark with permanent marker
I've made history like the Spanish Armada
You can't say that my style ain't harder, hot like Nevada
I ain't dead like the Wiley and Lethal saga, nah, I'm a leader
I lead the cattle like a farmer
See a girl once, she'll call me a charmer
Stage name's Wiley, my second name's Drama
I'm here for a laughter, just like Trimble
Centre court Wileys are done like Wimble
Albums doin' well so I want a grime single
Can't wait, I just wanna do my single
Why should I listen or mingle, with a label
That's not gonna do a grime single?
Stormy weather

When I merk one of them twenty man back it
You won't see me in a protection racket
I know the road's hard, I know you can't hack it
That's why I've got to teach you, always back it
Even if you're scared, I'll be there, I'll rack it
I'm a soldier, I'm older, I cause world traffic
Your crew won't manage but wait, don't panic
Go home and tell yourself you won't have it
Guns do bangin' it, I ain't sayin' go home,
Get a gun and come back and start bangin' it
But if you go that way and get the hang of it
My words to you will be, 'You're not havin' it'

F the western, F the system, I don't care
I've got my own system, are you listening?
The weather won't change, there will always be some
Stormy weather

That's why I'm still a fighter, the star in the sky
That shines brighter, the east side rider
Hyper like kitchen micra
It's a shame how people ain't tighter
We can be a powerful team so what we doin' then?
Everybody tighter, gotta be a fighter
I came from the drain so if ya come from there
Then push up your lighter
Look, there he goes, it's E3 boy
It's da 2nd Phaze, more peace for the boy
You're never gonna take no G's from the boy
Cos he ain't one of them boys, believe in the boy
There ain't no chief in the boy
He's got a lot of anger inside to release on a boy
That hates him for the wrong reason
Can't get along with the boy, don't chat to the boy

43. Eskimo Dance

Eskimo Dance used to be mad. It used to be properly underground. It all came from Sting, you know. The greatest one-night reggae and dancehall show on earth. Badman ting. When man just rush out and spray bars. Just mad.

Eskimo Dance had that kind of sound, it had that vibe, and it was a roadblock every time.

MCs would go down to battle each other; to have a clash. But it wasn't all aggro – spitting over a beat is how MCs express themselves. It's a form of poetry.

I think the real days are over, bro. Eskimo Dance has changed. There are no clashes. Everyone's scared of each other. People want five bags to battle. Money's not the factor, but bruv, when I used to go to Eskimo Dance back in the day, I had no choice but to think that any minute, my man is coming, and I need to be prepared. I've got to deal with it. But it's not the same. It's just not Watford any more, is it?

Mind you, SafOne reminded me of who I am. We done one in Birmingham – SafOne and a couple of the dons tried to rush the stage and bad up the dance. That woke me up. I realised, 'You're Wiley, bro. You're meant to be doing this.'

If we could go back to the old days, my ideal line-up? The Deja Vu mandem: Crazy Titch, Dizzee, Nasty Crew, Slew Dem, Boy Better Know. So that people get to see where it came from. But maybe when we're a bit older, when Titch gets out. A middle-aged man's Eskimo Dance.

44. £10

Janaya

Our mum always used to say, 'Have respect for money, and money will have respect for you.' It was a lesson Kylea took a long time to learn.

I know the value of money. I can remember not having any. When I lived in Romford, I had a job at a bank in Stratford. This was back in the early 2000s. Kylea was doing a lot of recording and a lot of performing, but there was very little money in grime, so I was basically supporting us both. It wasn't easy.

One day, he asked to borrow £10. I was broke. It was the end of the month, a Tuesday, and I wasn't getting paid until Friday. I had one £10 note in my purse, so I said no. But he begged: 'Janaya, I'll pay you back, I swear. Please.'

There had been talk of a record deal. But I only had £10 – £10 to last me three days! And I mean that was it. There was nothing else. No savings, no nothing. But he kept asking, and so I relented. I gave it to him.

The next morning I walked to work in the rain. From Romford all the way to Stratford. Eight miles or so. And no money for food, no money for a bus ride home. I wasn't happy, let me tell you. As I was getting ready to leave, a colleague came over and said that my brother had come to pick me up. He was outside with a few of his friends, laughing. He had just signed a solo deal with XL for a lot of money. A lot of money. That was the last time I needed to worry about £10.

Interlude

Crash Bandicoot

The way I stay live on a daily's crazy
I get short-tempered: don't talk, pay me
Turn to the dark side if my days ever get rainy, drain me,
    never not maybe
Yeah, I do know Jamie, and I know Sadie, her she's a cool
    young lady
Back to the way I live daily, had bare dough but that didn't
    change me
Yeah, I got a daughter, newborn child but her name ain't Amy
I ain't got a Winnie the Pooh scarf as yet, but I'm getting
    one, so stay away from me
I'll spray three-eighths and I'm not even crazy, not even lately
Don't fuck about cos you can't irate me
Wile Out ones don't know how to take me
Take out crews on a daily
I said I take out crews on a daily, standard
I done the dance more than your whole gang could
I swing through man just like Flow Dan would

I ain't from Brentwood, I come from Danwood
Straight from man-a-bad-man wood
Stand in flames, you could not cos you ain't from Danwood
Your whole plan would flop if you come across me and got
    lairy, standard

The bars I write they're like scriptures
I'm famous and everybody takes pictures
I had faith since decks and mixers
And you're a non-believer so I can't see you in the distance
Picture the game as a whole, healthy like the Boy Better
    Know T-business
J's my witness, I'm a musician, ask Skepta, three of us talk,
    we make a decision
You know me, I got good vision
Rudeboy, listen. Don't f about, there'll be a rudeboy missing
    when the goons start fishing
I'm an L-O-N kid, I got the hood snakes hissing
Me, the shotter that you couldn't really see, made the dream
    come true after years of wishing
After years of dissing, years of swinging
I still do the crime and walk, no singing

See the level I'm at, they wanna be at
The brake-horsepower's like a twenty-valve Fiat
There ain't a club that you won't see me at
Cos I'm a street star, there's no set time I have my tea at
You might see me draw a G at HSBC at Canary Wharf, retail
    therapy's me all week

Shot a key at, twenty-eight G at twenty past three

Twenty-seven, big achiever

E2 weaver

Had the first Sega

Blud, I emerged out of Jungle Fever, volume one creeper

Roman street sweeper

Don't get gash by the hour, rudeboy, I get gash by the metre

Wilehouse senior

Them all lean ya

E3 teacher

UK speaker

L-O-N preacher

Trinidad bloodline east side, that's where I ride, I'm a leader

East London Advertiser reader

Redwood bluewood, I'm a light sleeper

Stepney Green geezer

Ain't had shisha

I know Caroline but I don't know Alisha

I don't really care if either one of them done a ting with
    Josh, Perry or Peter

My love for them's nowhere on the meter

Eskidance keeper

Get the weed cheaper

Quantum leaper

The Tottenham High-Streeter

Eskibeat beater

A-star reader

Four-times community-service breacher

Back to court, facing jail: case beater
Robbery, burglary, dad got nicked cos of me
The police thought that I was a phone-shop dealer
Back in the day I was a wheeler and dealer
Fly to West where the sky is blue and the grass is greener
Paul Smith Jeans suit, Air Max Typhoon, chung gash greeter
Yeah, I know Jenny but I don't know Rita
My mum's family come from Antigua

45. Playtime Is Over

So me and Dizzee, we haven't really spoken in years. Since he got stabbed in Ayia Napa we haven't had a connection. I know that people wonder like, 'What happened there? Why they don't talk?' Or blah, blah, blah.

First of all, it happened because I took him to Ayia Napa. Our manager at the time told me, 'Do not take him to Ayia Napa. He's young. It's mad out there.' But I wanted him to come. Or, if he wanted to come, I wanted to take him. Why? Because he's Dizzee! That's our guy. We're going to Ayia Napa, we're gonna blaze up the mic, you get me? That's what I wanted to do. So we took him.

The situation happened. All very quickly. The massive, we're in a club and Dizzee pinched some girl's bum. This girl wasn't a nobody. She was there with two sets of street London people, it's not even a joke. It was so serious I can't even believe it. I'm not gonna lie to you. She was a woman from south London. She was not one of the Jezebels Dizzee talks about on his album. She's not.

Someone from our side came running over to tell me, 'Dizzee pinched so-and-so's bum.' But I was like, nah. This is nothing. But then I hear from one of the crews this girl was with. This man said, 'Oi, tell Dizzee I wanna see him.'

Maybe I was naive, but I didn't think it was going to be anything serious. I just thought it was still friendly, like we're going to see him, have a chat, sort it out, you know what I mean? So me and Dizzee left the club and go to talk to these people to sort it out. But as we walk up to them this man goes to slap Dizzee. Dizzee punches him back. Then we get rushed. By two crews. I may be exaggerating, but it felt like fifty, sixty people. And I don't mean like Jimmy and John and Jake, I mean name brands that I don't even wanna say, you know what I'm saying. Like, it was ridiculous, bro. Ridiculous. But like, there was no stabbing here at that point, you see what I'm saying. But there was no stabbing. He got hurt, and I got hurt too. Hence probably why the next day it carried on.

So the next day we go out to get some food, and two boys from one of the crews drive past on mopeds. I was like, 'Let's go!' – not really thinking. Just jumped up with the other boy we were with and chased after them. Dizzee stayed, which was probably the right thing to do. Anyway, so we get these boys, and get our own back a little, but now it's escalating. This is all men, young men, all egos, pride, beefing. You know what I'm saying? Something happened, something else happened, and suddenly it spiralled out of control. So we lost Dizzee after this. It turned out that he was out on his moped, and ran into another group of boys from one of the crews.

I wish he wasn't on his own when it happened. I wish he'd stayed with me. That's all I wish, because if he stuck with us, then it might have been a different story. You know what I mean? So after me and this other boy did what we did, they came back and found him. Just out in the wilderness.

This is the reason the manager did not want me to take him to Ayia Napa. That's it. And I didn't listen and I wanted to take him. I was like, shit, nah, his mum was going to be looking at me. The manager was going to be spiralling it up to try and make it look like 'See! I told you not to take him.'

It was a sad time, and it's never been resolved. Like I live in Cyprus right now, and it's all just there. I drive past the cemetery all the time. Or the clubs. Driving past around three, four in the morning and thinking: 'It was around now that it all started.'

But whatever, man, it's happened. It's happened, it's done and it needs closure. Every time I think of that whole situation, I cannot believe what went on. I can't believe that it's still the reason we don't talk today.

46. Badder Bars

Bro, I know when every single person on this planet is lying. It's not always a good thing either. You can be talking to your friend, they're lying to your face, and you know it.

Everyone's got a tell. Some people lie and they've forgotten what they said, and tell you something different. Other people have got nothing going on in their lives and say anything anyway, they just don't care about the truth. And with some people, it's in their body language. It's in their face. You start questioning what they've told you, how they've told you, even *why* they've told you. Sensing a liar isn't really something I've got a word for. It's an instinct.

You've got to remember that this industry is full of liars. Businessmen are liars. They lie and they hustle to get more money out of you, they put the lies in the small print, all sorts of shit. Gamblers are liars.

Basically everyone in this world is a liar. Your parents are liars. They teach you not to lie while they lie to you. Straight away, you're lied to when you're born. That's why the word exists. You've got to be able to sense it in other people, and move from them when they're lying.

I mean sometimes you can be wrong though.

*

People say that grime sort of stops or slows down when things are going well for us, which is true in a way. If you've got £27 million in your bank, then what have you got to be hungry for?

To be honest with you, I wouldn't know what to do if my life was perfect. Shit helps me with my creative process. Niceness doesn't. And since the day I was born, nothing's been right.

That's where the hunger comes from – the pain that I hold inside to do with me, my mother and my father.

I love them very much, but that pain can never leave me. A part of me will always be like, 'Jesus Christ, I wish I saw more of you.' I know other people have got it worse, some people have never seen their parents, so I've tried to forget it.

I know that the pain that's between me and my mother could last until we both leave this earth. But creating from pain isn't just darkness – I want to help my mum through it, I want to make her smile, I want to make her laugh.

Some people don't know how to channel their pain and use it to move forward. They just stand still, they drop on the floor. But I can't do that. I need to get it out. It's like an exorcism.

A song doesn't start in the world; it starts in my head. Nothing can come out of me if I've not gone through anything. Whether it's something good or something bad, I just need shit to be going on.

Back in the day it might have been that I was having a war on the radio. Or someone called me out, or someone wants to clash me. Someone tells me that someone doesn't like me. Fans are angry cos I didn't turn up. Something's not going right, and I need to make it right.

You can spit something good when you've planned it, but it's nothing like the raw lyrics you spit when your back's against the wall. My best lyrical moments aren't in songs. All my sickest bars come from warring.

The pain is where I'm coming from. If you haven't experienced pain, I don't know where you're coming from.

Grime is a rudeboy genre, all right, but it's not a badman genre. If you're a street don and you rep the streets, you know what the streets are about. They're not about grime. Some people work in the street, but a lot of people don't. And they don't have to. That's not who they are, and that's not what grime is. Your bars don't have to be bad. Your bars can't be badder than you are. You have to be badder than your bars. I can show you someone who makes the baddest music but hasn't lived a real day in their life. Dizzee got stabbed five times. You just have to be yourself. There's no point trying to be someone different.

Other people ain't like that. They don't come from pain. They don't come from anywhere muddy. Or guttery. Or dark. And you can tell.

*

Growing up in an atmosphere of violence fucks you up as a person, of course, but as a musician it can help you. It will give you that raw energy; that something to speak about. A smart person can channel it in a smart way, and it'll take you a long way. There's no story without pain.

47. Scoundrel

'Said I wouldn't do it a million times
Then I done it another million times
I can't talk no more I reply
When you move on I'm gonna want to die.'
Miss You

In my generation, no one knows what they're doing. Our parents' parents were different – they came from the West Indies to England to work. They just had to be on point.

But they had kids, and growing up in that time in London – my mum and dad's age group – meant that not all of them had their heads together. In the 1980s crack cocaine came in, and with the drugs came all kind of fuckeries. Poverty, violence, broken homes, kidnap, extortion. All kinds of fuckeries.

And men just fucked about. It wasn't easy for anyone back then – I've got no disrespect for them – but a lot of them are still not in a position to make money or save up for their family.

Our generation was worse. In my generation, people cheated fifty times a year. There was a lot of hiding and

lying. What I'm trying to say is that everyone was sort
of scattered back then, and our generation got much
crazier. We all grew up with a very negative attitude.

I've been a scoundrel, I'll admit it. I was cheating. I
was out there. A lot of men cheat. A lot of men growing
will have that phase. But some don't grow out of it. And
that's where the danger is.

   The truth is, even if you're in love, if you're out on the
streets, without your girl, you're single. That's what men
are like. And I'm only now getting to the age where I
realise what I've done, and I'm sorry for what I've done.
I understand how it can hurt.

   I was at my lowest when I split up with Lady Ny.
I loved her, but I hurt her. And then I saw her with
someone else. It was too much. It sent me a bit mad.

   I'm not a liar when it comes to music. I might lie to a
girl if I've cheated or whatnot, but never about music.

48. If You're Going Out I'm Going Out Too

Janaya

Kylea's a different man when he's in love. He's so polite.
Polite to the extreme. His girlfriends always told me how
much their parents liked him. He can turn on the charm
like that. And deep down, he's a very loving person. He's
a family man, you know.

Just to give you an example. He started going out
with this girl, and it was clear from early on that he
was really into her. She had family in Africa, so they
planned a trip to go out there and meet them. They
came round to my flat before they left, and I remember
he was wearing this huge silver necklace. Jewels,
everything. He looked good.

So they came back two weeks later or whenever, and
drove round to see me. I opened the door and the first
thing I noticed is that the necklace is gone. Instead he's
wearing this crusty little amulet thing on a bit of string.
And so is his girlfriend.

They came in, and we were talking, and it sounded
like they had an amazing time. He got on with her
family, as he would, and he loved the country. Wanted to
go back, in fact. So we chatted, and eventually I asked
about the necklace. 'Oh, he's so sweet!' his girlfriend
says. 'He saw them in a market and bought them for us.

They engraved our names on a grain of rice.' She walked over to show me – inside the amulet thing is a little grain of rice. I made the right noises, but I was thinking, 'What? This can't be real.'

I looked over to him and he's staring at me, a serious look on his face, but I knew he was trying not to laugh. 'That is so sweet,' I said. 'So where's your chain?' He was silently chuckling by now: 'Still in my suitcase.' I couldn't help it. I started laughing, and so did he. He had to leave the room. Luckily the kids were around, so his girlfriend didn't notice.

The thing is, he obviously meant it. It was a sweet thing to do. He's a romantic at heart. But I can just see through it. I wasn't laughing at her, just at him being this other person. And with me he couldn't keep it up.

He's an actor, I suppose. When he was younger, so many girls I knew would always say how nice he is, how he would be the perfect boyfriend. And I'd say, 'Yeah, for now. But give it a couple of months.' He's changed a lot, but back then, that was how it went. He'd be really romantic for a few months, and then something would switch. You know the song 'If You're Going Out I'm Going Out Too'? That's a good example of that switch. I should know. I laugh my head off whenever I hear that tune cos I remember him messing around that day. I was there when he had that argument with his girlfriend – maybe she was taking it more seriously than he was.

49. U Were Always

'*I need someone who's going to stand by*
I need someone who understands life.'
Special Girl

When I'm in love, I'll go to the ends of the earth for someone.

I'm not going to lie. I'm the best person when I'm in love, but I'm an utter wasteman if the girl I'm with has got friends who think they're clever and try to make me feel threatened. I've been an insecure lover before. So I've been with a girl – I love her, and she loves me – and when I connect with her boys, I can see that a boy wants to get with her. I know I shouldn't worry, but sometimes I just can't help it.

It's the way I came into life. I was never the first one to link the girls, that was always my friends before me. So there are always these rumours swirling around about who a girl had been with before, or what she might do next – all that stupid estate stuff. And the first girl I ever loved cheated on me.

Sometimes an insecure lover will cheat. You've had all these thoughts going round your head, you feel jealous, and then you think, 'Ah well, fuck it.' Then you're the one who's made the mistake. And when a man has done wrong by a woman, that's when she has to stand up and say, 'Nah.'

I think I was guilty of always trying to have one up on the woman. And how are you gonna stay the way you were at fifteen when you're older? You've got to grow and move on. You can't leave it too late, because the people who you've hurt along the way aren't going to be able to forget how you've carried on. Even if you're with someone who you've hurt in the past, don't get it twisted: they still know what you've done, it doesn't go anywhere.

When children are involved, you can grow to love someone. If a woman who you didn't love before bears your child, you can love her – trust me. Having a child with someone is a very special thing. It's a connection for life. It doesn't matter how rough you are with each other: when you die you will love her, and she will love you. It doesn't matter whether you're together or not. That's why it's so hard to be in another relationship when you've got children already. Especially for the first five years, it's almost impossible. It's not easy to stop thinking about somebody when you have had children with her.

Good-looking is just a preference; everyone has beauty. People ask the wrong questions about love. Don't ask yourself what your type is: ask yourself who makes your heart beat. Not just cos you're hungry for galdem, or whoever's considered the most pretty girl. People can look nice and be ugly on the inside, or the connection that you have with them isn't meant to last. Ask yourself who you see in your future.

To be with someone in the long term, you have to be friends with them first. When I had my first child, I lost the girl that I loved – but I gained the girl that was my friend. And that was a different kind of love altogether.

It happened after about a year and a half – of eating together, spending time together, and telling her everything that was on my mind. A female who is my friend will always get the truth from me, because I'm not trying to kiss her, or get her to lay down with me. With a normal girlfriend you fall into a routine, but with a friend you can be spontaneous. I could just ring her up and say 'Let's go here!' or 'I've got a couple hours free, let's hang out', and she'd be there at the drop of a hat.

Being her friend, I saw her character properly. I knew she'd be a good mum, even before she had my child, because I knew her as a strong woman. I could understand her without thinking too hard about it, because we'd be ringing each other up if we'd had an argument with whoever was our actual boyfriend or girlfriend at the time. Fancying the hell out of someone isn't the same as real love; it's not the same as getting to know someone.

*

'She knows Daddy ain't washed up yet
Cause I'm livin in the studio, lost, upset
When I find myself after all this music
I'll be watching her performing her set.'
Baby Girl

Parenthood is a lifelong thing. The best thing you can do
is raise your children.

There's no manual for this. You're not given a book at
birth telling you how to get on in life. You've just got to
have your shit together, by yourself. No one gives you a
guide called *How To Be a Parent*. I didn't have a normal
childhood growing up either. We grew up with our nan,
and she loved us, but it wasn't like having a mum and a
dad there. So, in a way, being a parent was foreign to me.

I was scared when I had my first child. I wanted so
badly for life for my children to be different to how it was
for me. But in a way I was always a dad to Janaya, so
I took to it in the end. I take them to school every day
in Cyprus. I look after them by myself when we're in
London. I want them to have structure and a normal life.

My girls love entertaining. They dance every day
after school. They want to go to America, they want
to go to this dance school there. They got Logic on
their computers and make a beat or two. They're more
active and ambitious than most adults! I want them to
experience everything that my life has to offer – cool
shows, new places, that kind of thing.

My dad always said that if a child does come along, that's a blessing. So you have to work around the blessing and still do what you're doing, but the person you're with, they'd have to understand that. If my job is a musician, for example, there's going to be a certain amount of being away and juggling things around. That's the nature of the business. I think my dad struggled with it too, when I was young. His way out of all of it was to take me to the studio, you know. Whenever he had an argument with my mum he'd grab me and say, 'Right, jump in the car, come on, we're going.' They were probably arguing about him not being around enough, so he'd pick me up and take me with me, just to say, 'OK but I'm taking him anyway.'

I think it's just kind of like my sister Aisha, because Aisha's like, she don't want to be the one always stuck at home looking after the kids, you know what I mean? There's got to be a balance. They wanna be out as well. I saw it in my mum, too.

I'm not a wotless father. I'm not one who my kids aren't gonna see. I'm not one who's run off from them and got another ten kids in Cardiff. I'm there. When you have a child, you have made a commitment for life. You've made a promise that for the next eighteen years, you are going to cover this child's back. That's the bottom line – whatever the budget, whatever the hustle, you've just got to do it. And every time you have another child, you're pressing the reset button on eighteen years of work.

I'm always going to be a father to my children. I will never turn left from them again. I will never be wotless. They're not gonna have the excuse of 'Oh, I never got to see my mum or my dad!' No – you saw both of your parents, and we're both here for you. There are kids who never got to see both of their parents, or only one of their parents, and they've still got their shit together. So I do expect a lot of my kids.

A lot depends on the culture that you grow up in. In the culture that I come from, children aren't planned. They just turn up. Sometimes the woman tells the man that she's pregnant and he gets with the programme, but a lot of the time a kid rocks up and they don't get to see their dad – ever.

This is where men slip up. When they're lying down with a woman, having sex, they're not thinking about those kids. In the back of a woman's mind she is, but maybe at that moment she don't care. And once it's done, it's done! I feel like adults should be more responsible and realise that when they lie down together, a child may be born, and take that seriously. But they don't. Adults are the most wotless people on this earth.

When I found out I was having my first child, I felt like I was going nuts. I had one gal here, one gal there, and all the rest of it. I knew I was going to lose all my galdem. The girl who was having my baby was my friend. I knew that I was going to lose my girlfriend, who I loved, when I told her what was going on. I was losing everything, but I had to get my head to where the children are. It was hard. You can't be with someone just because that's what you *should* be doing. It takes time.

I was in the pub every Friday with a lot of my white mates, and you know they have it large in the pub. I knew deep down that was wrong; being in the pub every night was not my thing, but I was trying to escape. It was fear. By the time my daughter was born, I was so far from normality. I was all over the place. But it had to happen that way: for something in my head to click and go, 'Look, you think you're Rico Suave, but this has to end now. You need to go and look after your child.'

To come back, I had to get away. My job is perfect for that: jump on a plane, become a tourist, disappear in another culture. It means I get out of my own head for a bit. I was in Sweden doing a show, and I had to get a train from one side of the country to the other. I was going through lots of green, lots of trees and peaceful landscapes, so I got to think a lot. I realised that I needed to get my shit together – that my daughter does not want to grow up and see me in the pub every Friday. My daughter wants a role model – to know that I love her, that I'm gonna look after her, and that I'll always be there for her.

50. £48,000

'Pour that money down the drain ... But that's another saga.'
I Just Woke Up

Janaya
The thing about Kylea is that he'll do anything for
people he likes. Money, time, whatever – for friends,
family, MCs. I think for him success is not measured in
how much he can get for himself, but how much he can
give to others. If he has something good, he'll share it.
He once gave a group of his friends £3,000 each for a
shopping trip, and then paid for all the clothes. He wants
everyone to feel equal. Even if his friends don't have a
lot of money in the bank, he makes sure they feel like
they do. He doesn't want anyone to feel that they were
any lower than he was. That's how he is. What people
don't realise is that he puts a lot of his own money back
into music. Most of what he earns he'll put back in. And
not just into his music, either. That's why his money will
go so quick.

He asked me to manage one of his bank accounts, so
I could send him cash when he needed it. He used to
call me all the time: 'Janaya, can you send me £5,000?'
It was his money to spend. He worked hard, he was a

success. Why shouldn't he enjoy himself? But it began to get out of hand. A lot of the money was for necessities – but a lot he just threw away. Once he asked me to book flights to Jamaica. He wanted to go on holiday. But not just him. He started giving me names – seven people in total. A lot of money. I said OK, and started looking online. He called me up two minutes later. They'd decided to bring along their girlfriends too. Fourteen return tickets. And he wasn't just paying for the flights.

'Have respect for money, and it will have respect for you.' At this point, Kylea had no respect for money whatsoever. He was stupid. He bought a Bentley and parked it on Roman Road. Somebody keyed it.

One day he called me from Manchester. 'I need you to pay our hotel bill,' he said. 'It's a lot.' £48,000. He'd taken over a whole floor of the Hilton in Manchester for a week. Parties, alcohol, food, everything. There must have been a lot of people, but he was the only one paying.

I decided to do something about it. He called me a few days later: 'Can you send me another £10,000?' I said no: 'You've only got £1,000 left. I'm serious.' He wasn't happy: 'There must be more somewhere?' I said no. He could have the £1,000 if he wanted, but that was all he had. He had to make do. And so he did.

I kept that up for a while. His account was beginning to look a little healthier. He rang me a few weeks later and said that he needed money for a trip to Cyprus. Could he have £1,000 or so? He didn't know it, but he'd just received a big royalty payment – about £25,000. So

I sent it all over. He was so happy. But he was a lot more careful with money from then on.

I think having children also had something to do with it. He wasn't in his twenties any more. He was getting older. He had responsibilities. He had a daughter to look after. He still lapsed, don't get me wrong, and he was still generous – but he had respect for money.

51. Shake a Leg

Scratchy

Wiley is the one who drives everyone to where they need to go, and he doesn't stop. He'll keep supporting you even when you've found success. He can't be happy in Harrods by himself; you've got to be in Harrods too. There's not a lot of humans like that, who'll help you without getting anything out of it themselves. It's because he wants you to share in what he's got – he wants you to reach his level, and take the baton off him and run with it. It drives me too. I look at his faith in me, and I want him to know that it's been for a reason.

The age gap isn't a gulf any more. We're peers now, it's like a family business. We need to show him that he wasn't wrong about us. I want to pay him back for everything he's given me in life. We're older now, we've got our business minds now, so it's time to step up. Like he got me a Yamaha R6 – it got nicked outside my house – and I want to be the one to turn around now and get him the R6. I want to support other artists the way he's supported me. I want to carry on his legacy.

It was Wiley who had all the ideas. He'd come in with an idea for a hook, or an idea for a beat, and we'd all jump on it. He was so far advanced, he could guide us through what we were doing with his vision. We were all really sick, but Dizzee and Wiley stood out as the special ones in the batch. Dizzee kind of kept himself to himself. The two of them had their own particular connection, I guess because they're both MCs. But they never showed a lot to people, they weren't going around like spudding or whatever. It didn't, to me at least, look as warm as what the rest of us had. I guess I stood out in my own way too – white boy, wild hair, all that.

Cutting the album with Roll Deep came natural to us. We'd be at the studio in Leroy Street every day – just ten of us hanging out, playing pool and making music. That's why *In at the Deep End* wasn't straight grime. We were experimenting, like with beats that weren't 140 bpm. Like yeah, you've got 'When I'm Ere', but tunes like 'Shake a Leg' and 'Avenue' reflect how much fun we were all having. We weren't actively trying to make hits, we weren't forcing it, we weren't worrying about the money. It was effortless. That's why my auntie will listen to it, your mum will listen to it, my nan will be in her wheelchair dancing like, 'Shaaaake a leg!'

I listen to 'Eskimo' still today. It's his oldest song, but that beat hasn't aged a day. His sound is different now, like it's as gully as it can be. I think he wants to prove himself again, to set the bar for everyone in grime again. I don't think he needs to. I honestly think *Godfather* is the best thing he's done. It's authentic. It's real. 'Speakerbox', from the beat to the lyrics, is perfect. And when he performs it live, he doesn't miss a single word. When he spits it's like a machine gun, and he doesn't skip a thing! I don't know other MCs who do that, they'd struggle in the rave if they tried.

I love them Roll Deep days, but even now, every time I see Wiley he'll do something that has me bussin' out laughing. He's not trying to be funny half the time. Like recently we were out in Cyprus, and even just driving down the road with him was hilarious. He was on the phone, and he was eating, and he was drinking some kind of slushy red daiquiri thing and bombing down the road with the boot of the car flying open! I was looking at him juggling this ridiculous ice drink in his hand, with chips in his mouth, and he just looked back at me like, 'What?' He's the most random breh.

I remember one night at Big Easy's. Me and Danny Weed had been drinking Zombies, and Wiley come along with twenty-one shots! We was absolutely fucked. He was working his way through the menu, got a Treasure Chest and everything. The whole night got blurry. I think we went to Janaya's house. But what happened there, I do not know. My memory stops at her front door.

52. Zombies

Janaya

Kylea laughed me into labour.

It was Friday night, 1st April if you can believe it. He'd gone out with Danny and Scratchy to Big Easy's in Canary Wharf. They were drinking Zombies, a cocktail we'd had together before, which are so strong that they'll only let you have two.

So obviously the boys had roped people into buying them more. I was at home with my son, and at midnight I heard banging downstairs. I opened my front door, and the three of them fell through.

We ended up talking for ages – about music, the scene, stuff like that. I remember laughing so hard I was crying, and I suddenly got this pain. Scratchy was saying, 'You're gonna be fine, don't worry.' The other two were just laughing their heads off.

The others left, and Kylea fell asleep. In the morning I wasn't laughing any more, the pain was so intense. And Kylea was still laughing, going like, 'Janaya, last night was so funny! It's sent you into labour!' I wasn't having it, saying, 'Just leave me alone, I can't talk, I need to get to the hospital.'

He was convinced that they were just going to send me straight back home when we got there, but two hours later I gave birth.

53. Representing

Jamie Collinson

I first started hearing about grime in the early 2000s. I'd been living in New York working as an intern for a record label, and then went off to Thailand, and so was completely cut off from the UK music scene for a while. When I got back to London Dizzee Rascal was on the front cover of *Jockey Slut* magazine and everything was changing.

I was very into rap music and hip hop, especially UK hip hop, but it always felt like there was space for something else, something that came more from black music and black culture in London and in the UK. Grime couldn't have existed without US hip hop, in terms of the stylings of it, and the attitudes and the behaviour, but it had a rhythm that audibly came from dancehall and jungle and garage. No matter how good UK hip hop got, it always felt like it was a US form at heart that had been adapted, whereas grime was a truly home-grown thing. There was always a lot of potential in UK garage, but I didn't like the poppy lyrics and sugary female vocals and shiny melodies, but I liked the drums and the bass. People like Wiley had seen potential in the darker, rawer things. And a lot of younger kids couldn't afford to go to the garage nights. It was all about getting dressed up and going out on a Saturday, everybody buying champagne and extortionate door fees.

I first started getting to know Wiley shortly after XL released *Treddin' on Thin Ice*. I read a piece on him that described the Eskimo sound – the glacial synth lines and icy electronic stuff – and it made it all sound very important. Home-grown and raw as hell.

A lot of grime wasn't very good on a technical level. I always thought it was a bit like a punk movement, where it was so DIY. 5 per cent of it was absolutely amazing and thrilling and 95 per cent of it was not, but it was exciting because people were trying new things, and everyone was allowed to have a go.

I first spoke to Wiley at Heatwave, a dancehall night. Riko Dan was hosting it one evening and Wiley was there with him. At that time I was running my own night at 93 Feet East in Shoreditch, and so I traded numbers with Wiley and booked him to appear. It was very nerve-wracking because I'd put him on the flyer, and he didn't used to turn up to things in those days. I remember standing behind the turntables on the first night and there was a crowd of people just standing there staring waiting for him to turn up and getting increasingly irate. And there was even this guy who I really didn't like from my university halls there, looking at me like 'You've fucked this up, haven't you?' And he even turned to leave, but then Wiley walked in and everyone went mad.

I started at Big Dada in May 2005, and at that point Wiley was shopping around *Da 2nd Phaze*. I think he had fallen out with XL, and I'd heard a lot of chatter about him being a difficult character. But I was young and keen and eager to do some grime. I was already interested in Wiley as a fan, and had become fairly friendly with him over text, so we decided to get him into the office. We got a bunch of demos out of him. 'Gangsters' for example. I remember standing outside Tottenham Court Road tube speaking to Will Ashon, the founder of Big Dada, about them. It was very exciting.

We seemed to have an immediate respect for one another. I'm not sure why, but we did. I remember him saying, 'You do know your grime, J. You're a white man from Leeds but you do know your grime, bruv.' For me, that was the moment he realised he could trust or like me. We had a very intense, largely text-message based relationship, and we started talking about when he might be working and where, and what might go on the album. He moved into Miloco studios in Elephant & Castle and I remember going to see him there while he was recording 'Playtime Is Over', the title track. But he had a falling out with Miloco – I remember them calling us up to say that he'd threaten to steal all the equipment, or torch the place – and so he moved into the Roll Deep studios in Limehouse, which was a golden little place for them all to record for a while.

He worked extremely quickly. We had a huge batch of album tracks quite soon. Everything has to happen very quickly otherwise he thinks people are bored and dragging their heels, and we were able to be quite nimble. We decided that we should have 'Gangsters' and 'Eskiboy' on there as they were such big recent songs. I would love to say that there's some A&R magic that went on with how the album came together, but actually the magic was probably not asking him to revise. He doesn't really like to revise things. If you said, 'This song is 70 or 80 per cent there, it could be absolutely brilliant if you do X, Y and Z', he'd say, 'No. You just don't like it.'

That was how the album was put together. There was very little sitting around in studios. It was more sequencing. I don't remember many disagreements. I wasn't sure about one or two of the tracks, 'Come Lay With Me' for example. We had a couple of philosophical discussions about that. But he quite rightly said, 'I'm black. I like black music. This is new jack swing. You don't get it because you're a middle-class white guy from Leeds.' 'Bow E3' was another one. Logan Sama for example thought that it was more of a mixtape tune. But it was pretty easy, really. We picked the songs we liked the most. You sometimes front load albums with the strongest songs, but there were too many to choose from on that album. It was all about doing something that was the best of its kind, and trusting that everyone could see that you were doing it, and could trust the product. We were committed to doing something that was exciting. We wanted to represent the genre properly.

Ewan Robertson designed the cover. He started as my intern in 2005. I remember him coming in very early on and saying that he was a graphic designer, and he wanted to design some covers, and I said, 'There's no fucking chance you'll be designing covers. You'll be making tea and stuffing envelopes and all of that shit.' And then of course it turned out that he was remarkably talented. So that was what he did.

The cover fitted the mood. It was a statement of intent and seriousness, but the black playground also captured the Eskimo sound, the playfulness, but also the frozen heart. I was very nervous about the shoot, because Wiley was nervous at that time about being on the streets. It wasn't just him. We had grime artists visiting Kennington who would be followed by local youths. It was genuinely dangerous, and Victoria Park, where we did the shoot, was particularly dangerous. There were all these Hackney gangs that would have been very keen to come across Wiley. He wouldn't have been able to walk around Hackney for five minutes without being set upon.

The scene was quite violent at that time, as well. There was his clash with God's Gift, and the clash with Ghetts, for example. There were stories around some of the people in the Roll Deep camp, for example. But I didn't really see it. Whenever I arrived at the studio it was like the teacher had turned up. Everyone was on their best behaviour.

With *Playtime is Over* there was a kind of catapult effect because Wiley hadn't done anything for a while, and he was elusive. The idea of a new album and him coming back was extremely exciting, and so there was a lot of noise around the album. I basically dedicated myself to accompanying Wiley to events all over the place. We spent a lot of time in Addison Lees. I remember going to the Ice Bar in central London to do the *Wire* cover, and he was like, 'It's too cold for me in here.' I think Lady Ny was with us, and she said, 'What are you talking about? You're supposed to be the Eskimo boy!'

Wiley was booked for the Splash Festival in Leipzig, which was a big German hip hop festival. Snoop Dogg was headlining. I went over with him. I was actually DJing for him for a while back then. The festival called up and said to him, 'Who do you want to DJ?' and Wiley just said, 'Oh, you can do it, J.' We drifted into Hackett at Stanstead Airport talking about the next album, and he was absentmindedly buying armfuls of shirts without looking at the sizes or anything. As we got through passport control, Wiley pulled out his passport and it was falling apart, the photograph hanging off. He'd put it through the wash. Obviously the customs officer wasn't very happy, but Wiley just wore him down. 'I ain't paying £80 for a new one, bruv.' The festival went well. Wiley had picked up some weed and so we had a bit of a wild night. Apparently Snoop had demanded that the festival arrange for various weed dealers to turn up at his hotel with spliffs for him to sample, and he'd bought a load from whoever had the best. Wiley had got some of it, too. That was a mad trip.

On the way back Wiley was wearing this crazy outfit – extremely loud shorts hanging low, one of his new Hackett shirts, sunglasses, gold teeth. As we walked through UK customs a respectable-looking old lady in front of us was pulled over and had her suitcase searched. Wiley was in hysterics. I said, 'What's so funny?' and he said, 'If you walk through looking like me they'll never pull you over. I've got Snoop Dogg's weed in my pants!'

Wiley is a star, in that he changes the atmosphere in a room as soon as he walks in, and all of those other clichés. It felt like we were building a wave of something, and it was all really fun. And *Playtime* was a success. It sold well, and got a lot of noise. He was getting some pretty big royalty statements before too long, as well as money from publishing. He actually gave me one of his publishing cheques. I said, 'You know I'm getting paid for this, don't you?' But he said, 'I always said I'd give you something, J.'

After *Playtime* we did another single, but that was it for a while. He just said, 'I can't be trapped by a label. I need to go and be a popstar.' That was how it was with him. He'd veer between needing to make a grime album, and achieving some level of mainstream success.

Which is understandable, considering the advances he can get from the major labels. And Wiley has been signed to every major label at least once. From the time of Pay As U Go when he spent all his money cabbing his friends around London. I remember he said he went into one label for a meeting, and the executive said, 'I can't believe you're sitting in the chair in front of me again. You've had a lovely run, ain't ya?' This guy had been giving him advances since he was seventeen. But he could probably say it's frustrating working for a label like ours where you don't have the budgets or all the major label trappings.

We made it clear that we were keeping the door firmly open, and I stayed in contact with him. We kept texting, with the odd meeting or two. It was always weird conversations out of car windows and in studios. We wouldn't sit in a bar and have a drink, or that kind of thing. But we kept in touch. There was a lot of affection there.

54. Cash in My Pocket

From 2007 or 2008 to 2013, I just had to make money. I had to feed my children. I still made grime, but I knew that it wasn't selling. When I first came through, I wasn't that sensible. 'Come on lads, let's go to LA.' 'Come on lads, let's go West End, spend £20,000 on clothes.' And then all of a sudden, I realised I didn't like zero.

That period of time was the John Woolf years. John Woolf at his best. He's got a skill. He can walk into somewhere, have a conversation, do good business, come home, and we all get paid. And in the evening we're drinking wine, we're eating olives, and cheese, and crackers. Managers need to be able to walk into a room and get deals done, and that's what he did. Between 2008 and 2013, any fuel I gave him, he went out, and did the job.

I always tried to do a little thing for the chart, and then go back to grime. I was trying to push grime onto the people who liked 'Wearing My Rolex'. But what I came to realise is that it doesn't work, in the long term. If I never made pop tunes I might not have made it through. It was me doing stuff I didn't really want to do. But I knew what to do. I listened to the radio. So I just thought, 'Oh shit, you know what. Sample these old guys, bust a one Chas and Dave, you know.' The art is trying to reach all these different people, and in England, whatever the biggest thing is, is what they see you as. If you've got a big song, that's what you're known as. Say I had a big pop hit, and put out ten other grime tunes, they will only know you for the pop. I was never going to win that battle. So in 2013, I think we made 'Lights On', with Angel and Tinchy, and I didn't want to do that single at all. I thought, I'm done. My major label pop period is done. I'd given at least six years of my life to it. Quickly jabbing a single in there, quickly grabbing some money, trying to sell grime.

*

'Labels say that you can have control but labels lie a lot.'
Talk About Life

I've had a few tricky relationships with record labels. Some I love, but some were just terrible. They say you need to have a label – but you really don't. And today a lot of artists realise that. Today more people are doing it on their own, and doing it well. Look at BBK. Look at Stormzy. You work at your own pace and you realise your own vision. Not someone else's.

I've signed with one label and not put anything out. Nothing. Took the money and moved on. Not to cheat them or anything like that, but just because what they wanted and what I wanted were worlds apart.

One example, yeah. Back in 2008 or whenever, I wrote 'Cash in My Pocket', recorded two verses and handed it over to the label. But for some reason, they wanted three verses. It made no sense, bruv. They kept pushing. The label was calling, John Woolf was calling, but I just thought, 'They'll leave it.' In fact, I told John to leave it as it is.

The next thing is they've sent me the final cut and added another verse, some freestyle from way back. John has set them up with it. So I lost it. I don't moan at John Woolf for no reason. I moan at him because he told me one thing, and in reality it's another thing.

I hated myself for chasing those deals. You can get money to cover yourself easily, through touring or whatever.

Look at what happened with *The Elusive*. Me and Island were battling over what that album should be. Fifteen, sixteen songs or something? We couldn't get near. But I had two hundred songs on my computer, just waiting. That is something I can't handle. I was tired of waiting for the deal.

In the end, I didn't care about the album any more. I was nothing. When no one is listening to me, I'm nothing. I'm just in my own little world going mad. It made me feel sick. I thought, 'Send it out, start again. Make better music.' So I leaked it all. It's my work. You're making money, but it's my work. Nobody fucks with that.

And I ended up getting another deal anyway.

There was one guy in particular I really didn't get on with. Quite high up in one big label. We'd released a single, and something had wound me up, so I called him and told him that I was going to come through and ransack the office. They were empty words – I was just angry, I wasn't being serious, but he took it very seriously.

They took it too far. I think they even got the police to come and guard the building. Then the guy even left the country. Maybe on holiday or whatever, but he didn't want to come back. He'd ring John and say, 'Is it safe yet?' John didn't really like this guy either, so rather than setting him straight, he'd say, 'You know what? I don't think so. You'd better stay away for a little while longer.'

55. What Goes Around

'Wearing My Rolex' was the highlight of my whole career. People forget that for a long time grime didn't really pay. I had to do all sorts of shit, and focus on whatever did pay. If that's considered selling out, then that's what I did. That's what had to happen. 'Wearing My Rolex' brought me a lot of money. I made more money from recording one song than I earned in many years of making grime.

But it was like my biggest success was poisoned. I got so paranoid about being in Bow, about certain people that wanted a piece of me. Not just the money or the fame, but actually wanted to do me in.

There was this proper old-school East End gangster, and he wanted me to help his son get into the music industry. So I tried to book some studio time for him, but for whatever reason I couldn't do it. It was booked up or something. No big drama. But they kept calling to ask me what was happening, and I might have been a little rude.

They didn't stop ringing me. They wanted to meet up. A guy I knew was speaking to them, and said I should go along. So I did. There were a few of them, and it was obvious that they were angry, that they felt I had disrespected them for not letting them use the studio, and for the way I spoke to them on the phone.

Nothing happened until the very end. They got this guy I trusted to grab me, hold me down. And that's when it happened. Someone came over and slapped me on my cheek. Just a slap, but he had a blade hidden between his fingers. When he slid his hand back, my face opened up. I was slashed from ear to chin.

My manager rented me a house in Kent straight away, got me security and drivers and all kinds of things. I just didn't feel safe any more. I didn't do the 'Wearing My Rolex' video because I didn't want people to know where they could find me. I didn't want to show my face.

How can the tabloids say it's cos I'm scared of foxes, or that I'm unreliable? It was like salt in the wound.

I could've done what Dizzee did – just leave for ever. But I had to come back to Bow, I had to show my face in the ends. I have to know what's happening. John would love me to hide away in some huge mansion in Kent, but I need to be in the mix. That's what makes me happy. That's what makes me Wiley.

I'm never going to be a grass. I was never going to go to the police, and John found it a bit strange at first. But it's better karma that people have to live with themselves after doing what they done. I've gone on to be even more successful. That kid never got anywhere in the industry. And the man who held me down ended up in a bad way. What goes around comes around.

1. Me and my aunt June in 1979

2. Me (right), my mum and cousins

3. Me, my auntie June and cousin Damien at June's wedding in Poplar, east London, 17 May 1979

4. Me, my aunties, uncles, cousins and grandparents at my nan's house

5. My uncles, aunties and cousins at a family wedding

6. Leader of the pack!

7. Me, my dad and my sister, Bow E3

8. Bow skyline: Clare House is on the right

10. Jammer's staircase

9. Deja Vu, back in the early days

11. Wiley vs Kano: one of the biggest clashes ever

12. Eskiboy

13. The three blocks. Me and Dizzee, back at the beginning

14. Camera crew at the Wilehouse

15. Early promo shot for the first album

16. Rolling Deep!

17. *Treddin' on Thin Ice* album cover

18. *Playtime is Over*. Shot in Victoria Park by Ewan Robertson

19. Mandem at the MOBOs

20. Me and Jammer

21. The video for 'Numbers in Action'

22. Pure fire!

23. Eskimo Dance take to the stage at the Red Bull Culture Clash

24. Me and Skepta at the *Godfather* Roundhouse show, 2017

25. My plaque at Bow School: 'The whole of E3 got so much talent I hope you see'

26. Suited and booted at the Brit Awards, 2017

27. Picking up my Lifetime Achievement Award at the NMEs, 2017

56. Know Your Mind

Trust isn't an easy one for me. I suppose most people feel happy handing over responsibility or money or whatever based on a quick meeting, a few calls. For me it takes years. If it ever happens. That's not just professionally – I mean personally too. In my life there are only a few people I feel I can really trust. It might have something to do with my upbringing, or maybe what I've been through. I've been through a lot, you get me.

Everyone I looked up to in my entire life has disappointed me. Everyone.

An MC cannot be held responsible for what they say. Bring up your kids the best way you can, and hope that they're not stupid enough to just follow what people say. My advice is: kids, don't look up to no one. Just be your own self. Know your own mind. If I jump in the fire, you're not gonna.

Janaya always said that if the person who brings you into the world can't be there for you, who can? My mother wasn't there when we were small. She left me and my sister with our grandparents in Kent. It was my grandmother, really. My grandad didn't really have time for kids. Even when he was there it was like he wasn't there. My grandmother was good, but she was fierce. And she wasn't my mother. It was just me and Janaya, really.

I can't blame my mother for leaving us like that. I
don't know what she was going through, with what
happened to her brother. Can you imagine looking after
two babies after that?

Saying that, Janaya also thinks it has something to
do with me being a Capricorn. I don't know.

I work in a world where you've got man who just want
to see you down. When I was living in Bow, people would
knock on my door and try and rob me. I guess you can't
be in the hood with that kind of dough. I'm blessed now.
I'm a big man, I'm old. I'm not in the spotlight like the
younger ones. These people – they don't want a big man.
They want the kid who's popping. I can go to Nando's
and flex. But I remember the times.

One of the worst things that ever happened to me was
organised by someone I trusted. A friend, you know.
From Bow. From time. He helped set the whole thing up.
And you can't do anything about it. If that happens, you
think you're going to be ready to put your life in some
next man's hands? Not any more. And now I've got even
more to lose.

Basically if I think you're a mug, I'll treat you like
a mug.

Handle Ya Business

If you've heard me for too long, can't hear me now
Yo, I get it, can't get a vibe near me now
It's a past thing, you won't like me
Even if my next thing's better than my last thing
Cos that's blessed
All I gotta do is make sure that my level stays higher than
    the rest
Put a legacy to rest
And I give that a good send-off, I'm a top don here, end of
Good and bad's what I'm a blend of
Me and Scratchy D been about like Shifty and Remdog
Clear brudda from a day one
I get the bread in my old age, wha' ya mean crumbs?
My hunger's like this cos I came from the slum
World's going too fast so it's weed that I bun
Since '99 man have had a great run
I live life in the snow, I live life in the sun

I can make your life fun
Amazing taste, I'm like Stardough
My whole career, that's all a work of art though
Show me to a sign that says 'Start Job'
Beats getting vocalled here or getting parked off
There's a few circles of music that your boy Wiley will never
be a part of
I like to put work into an artist's career before the ting
starts off
Handle ya business right
Keep your team so tight nobody's gonna fight
Yo, handle ya business right
Forget friendship here, that's not what it's like
Yo, handle business correctly
I'm clued up eight years after John Woolf met me
Handle ya business carefully
When I move round in the group, cos nobody airs me

I ain't got a price any more, just like
I ain't selling, I'm only buying
At the start of the game I was only trying
My life's plain now, bro, like I'm only flying
Somebody told you my bars are dead, but
Ha-ha, they was only lying
I get wins round here, and some take L's
While the other dons out here are only tying
I said my flow is in front of the pack
Yes, I rang Dizzee up when I wanted a pack
Target taught me when I wanted to stack

Kelvin and Bodie had us wanting to rap
All my olders had man running the trap
Whatever got stole they'll be runnin' it back
I ain't lying, whatever got stole they'll be runnin' it back

Yo, image ting, everyting fresh
I should put diamonds in a bulletproof vest
I got my scene doing bits for the team so it ain't gonna
    matter when you put us to the test
I make a doubter eat his words and feel shitty
Came from the roadside like Po Nitty
Might buss a hat when my hair gets picky
Then I get a haircut then the galdem see me

Everyting's on fleeks
I set the pace then you follow like sheep
I got more money than my log-ins
And when I talk, my talk ain't cheap
When Titch first popped I was there
When JME first popped I was there
When Stormzy first popped I was there
And I'm still here today after all these years so…
Image ting, got it on lock
Had it on lock before Tinie popped
Had it on lock before grime was hot
God knows, bro, it's my time to win
And we all know now it's your time to cotch
It's in my veins, that's why I can't stop
Walk in the studio, I know myself

When you walk in the studio the stuff stays off
Now, image ting, make it look good
Even if you ain't, make yourself from the hood
Even if you weren't there, put yourself there
I can see when a brudda's being boog, good
So I should, because I got brains, I'm the main man
All of the shit, it was my game plan
Fame came to me, I was popping like Ray-Bans
I run shit when I'm here like my name's Giant Haystacks
Run revenge, run payback
If one per cent of you doesn't like me when I'm spraying
    bars then, bruvva, stay back
You can't spray up me because I'll spray back
And when I spray back? Lord ha' mercy
Some of them dubs them are percy, flows too perky
You don't want beef, you're a jerky
None of your bars are gonna hurt me

Bro, you move too slow
I was on Z when you was on O
I was on ten when you was on one
Every dance I spray the dance dem dun
Take a walk with me, talk sport with me, come to court with me
Help Donny get on and when he got on
Went his way and never thought of me
I ain't hating, but that's not cool to me

Image ting, everyting fresh
I should put diamonds in a bulletproof vest

Got my scene doin' bits for the team so it ain't gonna matter
    when you put us to the test
I make a doubter eat his words and feel shitty
Came from the roadside like Po Nitty
Might buss a hat when my hair gets picky
Then I get a haircut then the galdem see me

57. Wearing My Rolex

One of my sickest verses is on 'Holy Grime' with Devlin, for sure. But the smartest song I have ever written, in my whole life?

It's 'Wearing My Rolex'.

'Wearing My Rolex' took me half a second to write. I didn't even have to try. It was like going to school and not doing any work for an hour, just messing about. And it's my biggest tune.

It's not my favourite tune. I could write a song that is kerrrrazy. Intricate patterns, spitting a mile a minute, all of that. But the crowd might not sing it back. There's nothing in the world like a crowd chanting your words back at you.

I didn't have to say much, but they understood me.

58. Woolf

John Woolf is a powerful figure, don't get me wrong. He can walk into any office and get money. Not many people can do that. People respect him. I respect him. He'll always show up. He can move in places that maybe I can't. He's been there for a long time now. He's family.

I don't know what he thought would happen when we first met. This was just before 'Wearing My Rolex'. I'd asked Twin B and Richard Antwi to recommend me a manager, someone who was good with money. He'd done some stuff with the Roots, was friends with Mark Ronson. He'd been on the scene for a while, anyway, and sounded good. So I got them to bring him to some cafe in Hoxton.

He walked in and sat down, and I was like, 'So you're my manager now.' And he looked so surprised, like I was being strange or something. He had this whole speech prepared about how you shouldn't just jump into these things, that a relationship with a manager is like a marriage and dah di-dah di-dah. I was just like, 'Erm, no, my mum told me I needed a Jewish manager and so you're my manager now.'

Four weeks later we put 'Wearing My Rolex' out, and we were battling Madonna to be top of the charts. My mum was right.

59. Wiley

John Woolf

Madonna only beat us because she had Justin Timberlake and Timbaland on the same song, which is basically cheating.

It was such a crazy time. I can only remember meeting him that first day in flashes, because it all happened so fast. I couldn't believe he wanted me to manage him without knowing anything about me. After the meeting he got me to give him a lift to somewhere random in Bow. He jumped out the car and was like, 'You're my manager!' and I was just sitting there a bit stunned, feeling a bit weird.

It took a while for us to understand each other. I had to learn to navigate him, and not to take things so personally. There are ups and downs that come with him, and he has that reputation for being a bit difficult.

We had an issue when doing a song, 'Cash in My Pocket' with Mark Ronson, who's a friend of mine. Wiley had done two verses on that song, and for some reason just wouldn't do a third verse. Someone at the label told me they simply couldn't release the track with only two verses. But he'd done an absolutely incredible freestyle on something else. So we pieced it together on 'Cash in My Pocket'.

Back then there wasn't Twitter, but there was something called Rewind Forum. He was always so alert, even from when we were doing 'Wearing My Rolex', to people calling him a sell-out or this or that. I would be like, 'Do you care what adidastrainers16 who lives in the middle of fucking nowhere thinks about you, or the 200,000 people who've gone out and bought your single?' But there was always a part of him that was sensitive to what those keyboard warriors had to say.

So when it came to putting this verse on 'Cash in My Pocket', he just went crazy. He spiralled out at me and the label and everyone. I suppose, looking back on it, there's a lot that I'd do different now. It's easy to say that after ten years with someone. Regret isn't really in his vocabulary. Wiley lives in the moment, and then he moves on. He doesn't dwell on things. And to be honest, that's what I love about him. There's no filter – he says what he thinks. He doesn't want to play the game of censoring himself. Twitter was the best and worst invention for him.

Wiley's got a habit of savagely berating people online. I've honestly lost count of the number of times he's 'fired' me. And then he'll call me like nothing's happened. But it is what it is, and we've just got to keep it moving. What people don't realise is that when he's on Twitter calling me every name under the sun, he's in my house asking me for a glass of orange juice! He's like two different people – Richard can be in your living room, chattering away politely, while Wiley's on Twitter wanting to empty a full clip into you.

He's got that line on 'Handle Ya Business' – 'I'm clued up eight years after John Woolf met me' – and I think that's because he used to be very reckless with money. He'd take Addison Lee cabs from London to Edinburgh, or book them and get them to wait around for him outside festivals. For hours and hours. I once got a bill of £20,000 for one trip. When someone's young you can try and advise them, but who wants to do the boring stuff like invest in bonds and property? It's just not exciting. I wish I could go back in time and change that – in the time I've known him he's spent obscene amounts of money, like probably millions. But now he's older he wants to be responsible.

If he wanted to he could have signed Dizzee. He could have signed Chip, Tinchy, JME, Skepta. He could have been the head of a Def Jam in the UK! But maybe it was a lack of business savvy, or he just didn't want to sign his friends or something like that. He'll give people money for studio sessions, for flights here and there, and never ask for it back. I'll be like, 'Where's the money? Is it ever coming back? What the fuck?!' But he doesn't want to have power over them like that. He wants to see people do well with no gain for himself. I think he missed a trick there. But now he sees that by virtue of his reputation that he can get young artists attention by signing them, like this guy Margs. He can get on the radio now, he can move in the spaces that'd be closed to him if he was on his own.

Hindsight's a beautiful thing, and maybe if he hadn't done those things that hampered us he'd be bigger than Stormzy and Skepta. But he's a maverick. He's a genius. He's not gonna play by the same rules. You never know what's coming with him. I'd probably have a much easier life managing Michael Bublé, but would I actually be happy working with someone that vanilla? And the relationship has mellowed as we've both got older.

We share the same goals – keep him current, keep him ahead of the curve, and keep him from being some kind of Radio 2 act. It's been almost twenty years since 'Nicole's Groove', so it's about defining a legacy. We've got our own personal Everests we still want to climb – like touring America, or getting him to the O2 Arena on his own. I want that moment of being able to look down and say, 'We've won.'

60. Bad Songs

I've made a couple of bad songs. John Woolf music.

Saying that, in some ways, 'Heatwave' is my favourite. It's the one that's done the most for me. It's gone to number one. It's like a saviour record. Every time I listen to it now, I remember what happened when it was released. I'm like 'Wow!'

I don't like them years though. I don't like them because my country bigged me up for them and then shat on me for them. So I don't like them.

For every one person who was like, 'Yeah, man, "Rolex"!' there would be another five saying 'You sell-out', 'That's shit', 'What the fuck did you make that for? You should've made grime.' All I could say was, 'Err, no one listens to grime right now. You're all in fucking house raves and garage raves.' Then they'll be like, 'Yeah, but that doesn't mean you should switch,' and I'll be like, 'You know what, I've got two kids. However I can make money I'm gonna do it. I love grime but I'm in the minority right now. The majority of this country likes this.' And that was just the people who said things to my face.

So if I want to make money quickly I'm gonna do that. If I didn't make those songs I would have been broke from 2008 to 2013. It seemed like some people were more angry that it was popular. If those songs didn't work, I'm not sure I would have the same kind of response.

One thing it's taken me a long time to realise is that you can't please everyone. If you don't know what you're talking about then shut up.

At one point I nearly went on *Celebrity Big Brother*. They'd offered me a ridiculous amount of money to do it, we were having a bit of a quiet period at that time and I was very, very tempted. John had actually negotiated a contract to the point where it was ready to sign. I even had an escape clause: if I jumped the fence after twelve hours or whatever, we'd still get the cash.

But in the end I turned around and said, 'Nah, I'm not doing this. It'll kill us.' So John said, 'What next?' I went away and made 'Heatwave' and handed it over. Straight to number one.

It could have been some good TV, though ... I heard this song, 'Cheap Thrills'. It goes something like: 'I don't need no money, I don't need dollar bills to have fun tonight.' And I was thinking to myself, 'Of course you don't need money, you nutter, you've already got it – everywhere you go you probably don't have to pay anyway.' And these people are actually millionaires, do you know what I mean?

*

I have never made a classic album. I've made classic music, maybe. But not a classic album. Don't get me wrong, I could take you to my house and play you eighteen best tunes, they'd be hard. But projects I can't do. Because I've done so much different shit. I'm too experimental for me to be able to stop and say, 'That one was classic.'

A classic album should be a bible and a blueprint. It should set the bar, and set a model for others to follow.

I don't think I'm an album artist. I've never had a successful album. I only know how to make music. I've never gone gold. I've never had an album to say 'Yes!'

I made enough money there to fund whatever I wanna do. And every time I'm doing pop or I've done pop, I've spent most of the money I've made on grime anyway. It's not necessarily about the money you get, it's about what you do with it. I believe in helping people out. Nothing bad ever comes from it, only good. I think that's why I lasted for so long. I'm tired now, but I've lasted for quite long. On that principle.

61. Slippin

Wherever I go, I always feel like I have to get to know it. A hotel room is not good enough. And if it's somewhere I like, I might stay.

I moved to Liverpool for a bit, to Birmingham, to Manchester. At first it was to get away. I was young and rich. I had an Aston Martin and a Bentley. I had more cash than I could handle, but I was still living as if I was fifteen. I thought that nothing would change, but you can't live in Bow and flaunt your wealth like that. I love Bow, it's a good area, but people don't like you rubbing their noses in your money. Some people criticised me, people wanted to borrow from me, some people wanted to rob me. In Manchester, everything was cool. I could drive around the city, park where I liked, no problems.

After that, I just got the travelling bug. Australia, for example. I'd done this big Australian tour, and spent quite a bit of time in Western Australia. Skepta came out for part of it. I loved Perth, I remember. Perth is sick. So when the tour was over, I went back. John called me up and was like, 'Where are you?' I said I was spending a few days in Perth. To be honest, it's a long flight back, and I needed a break. But I stayed for two months.

What do I do? I just get to know the place. Rent a house. Drive around. Find out where to eat, where to get your hair cut. Get family over. Just living.

I've done it a few times. Toronto, I loved. That was mad. After I was banned from the US, that was my place. Canada was a taste of the vibe. I was so happy when I got through, I stayed there for six months. And Cyprus. I've got a good little set-up in Cyprus as well, good enough so that I can go work and come back and just chill. But we've got family all over.

I bought a flat in Rotterdam. My auntie lives over there. I loved it, so I just said, 'Let's find something.' Life is good. Get a bus to Amsterdam, buy the best burgers, you know. And all the local producers are into grime. I even did a track in Dutch for them. Man learnt Dutch!

Jamaica, too. Jamaica was something else. The first time I took my sister to Jamaica I said to her, 'Listen, we can't stand out. We've got to act like we live there.' She was packing all her clothes, everything. I said no: flip-flops, leggings and T-shirts, that's all you need. That trip was sick. One day I was out with my sister in Kingston and I got a call from this producer to come to the studio. We was close to where he was, so we meet up, and he says he'll take us to this place, right in the middle of the ghetto, you get me. Just wandering down these lanes, people looking at us. My sister was scared, she was like, 'Let's go!' But I thought this was real

life – this was where the real people were. So we get to
the studio and everyone is there, Vybz Kartel, I even
think Bounty Killer was there at one point.

It's important you don't just take, just go to an area
and use it. I had my own little studio in Jamaica for a
while and there was this kid who used to hang around
outside. Should have been in school, but I don't know
what was happening. We got to know him and he was
into music and whatnot. He liked what we did. So I said,
'Next time we're here, come in, jump in the booth. We'll
see what you can do.'

Anyway, one thing happened, and then another thing,
and then before you know it we were supposed to be
flying back. On the last day I said to my sister, 'Let's
just go back to the studio quick. I've got to see this boy.'
She was like, 'No. Time to leave.' And we had no car –
we had given it back. But I had made a promise. The
studio was a lot further than I thought, up hills. But
we get there, and the boy is waiting outside. We made
a couple of tracks, good tracks, and got the plane. I still
speak to him.

62. More Life

Janaya

He likes having people around him. He doesn't like
travelling by himself. That's why I got to go a lot of places;
he'd say, 'Do you want to come to Ireland? Do you wanna
come here, do you wanna go there?' and I'm like, 'Yeah, of
course, I'll come.' Because I used to manage his bookings
one time as well. When I was about nineteen, I used to
get all his bookings for him and stuff so I used to go to all
the trips, but if he's with an entourage of people he don't
mind because he likes adventure. He's like a big kid. But
it's also about security. If you've got a team around you,
then you've got backup in case anything happens.

Not long ago I was out with my brother and Danny
Weed. We went to a Turkish restaurant in Bexley
Heath. I think this was just after Kylea had got back
from one of his trips, and he was telling us about it.
Danny said, 'Will man, you've got to stop going on these
adventures! We need to calm down, we're getting old.'
My brother was like, 'No, Dan, you're only as old as you
feel. You're acting like you're sixty, blud!' Two minutes
later, he decides to go to Toronto, and asked Danny if
he wanted to come along, as if the conversation hadn't
happened. Danny was like, 'I can't just pick up my stuff
and go to Toronto! What are you talking about?'

That's just how he is. All the time: 'Let's go here! I know, let's go to Jamaica! This is happening! That's happening!' My mum used to drive around with her passport and a suitcase in her car just in case he'd ring. There's no time to plan – you have to be ready. My sister used to say, 'How comes I never get to go nowhere?' And Mum would reply, 'You can't sit around and think about whether you wanna go or not, you've got to go. You've got to be ready at the snap of a string.'

Like he'd ring my mum and say, 'I'm on my way to Gatwick. If you can get here by half past seven you can come too.' No mention of where they're going. And Mum would be like, 'Oh, I've got to go, grab my stuff! Where's my passport?' and we were trying to get her to calm down. But she wouldn't listen: 'No, because if I get there late, I've missed the boat.' She likes spending time with him, and she has a bit more freedom. My dad's always busy, so he can never go. But he's spontaneous too. I'm sure there's a part of him that would love to go every time Kylea calls, but he can't.

I had a similar experience when he went out to Toronto. He went there for a show, but he liked it so much he just stayed. He'd met somebody who was renting out these two apartments in a building where a lot of basketball players lived. It was like a hotel – like on top of the Hilton hotel. After a week or so, he called me up out of the blue and said he'd got me and my son a ticket. He said we could have this second apartment.

He rang me, like, 'I've got you an apartment. Your flight's at this time,' and I said, 'Kylea, are you mad? I can't just leave,' and he was like, 'Nah, you've got to come here, quickly, get yourself.' He said, 'Don't pack anything, just bring an empty suitcase and we can buy everything new when you get here. Just don't miss your flight.' I had about two hours to get to the airport. I just went.

I remember my son's dad came round to say hello just after I'd left. He's like, 'Are you in? I'm just outside,' and I said, 'Oh no, sorry. I'm on my way to Toronto.' He's like, 'You what? I know you're joking.' An hour or so later he FaceTimed me: 'Janaya, where are you?' and I was like, 'I'm at the airport. Look!' and he still couldn't believe it. I said, 'I'm going to have to go, otherwise I'll miss my flight.' He was like, 'Well, OK. How long are you going for?' 'Five days,' and he went, 'All right, cool.' Five days. I stayed for three months.

But that journey was a nightmare. We got on the plane in time, and arrived in Toronto no problem, but they wouldn't let us through customs. My son doesn't have the same surname as me, and so they didn't think he was mine. In Canada and America there's a lot of child abduction, apparently. They said, 'Well, if you're his mum, why hasn't he got the same name as you?' What could I say? 'He is my son. His name's got nothing to do with it.'

But they needed proof. They started questioning me. They asked who I was there to see, and I had to explain that my brother had just arrived, and bought us tickets to come out. They found that quite difficult to believe. Then they started talking to my son. He was only two or three at the time, and couldn't say very much, but they kept asking him who I was, and for some reason, he kept saying 'Janaya'. He knew my name, so he was just answering their question. I couldn't say anything to him. They were like, 'You've got five hours until the next plane back to London. Unless this kid says "Mum" before then, you're both going to be on it.'

Meanwhile, Kylea was on the other side of the airport waiting to pick us up. He kept calling, and eventually they let me answer. 'What's taking you so long? I've been out here for ages, man!' I said that I was being held in customs because of my son's name, and he started laughing his head off. Then I see him tweeting it, as we were talking. I said, 'Why are you putting it on Twitter!' And he was like, 'Fathers have rights, too!' I was so embarrassed.

I told them to get hold of my son's dad as well, to verify who I was. So they called him, and I remember they got through and they were like, 'We have a Janaya Cowie in customs.' They put it on loudspeaker and he was laughing his head off and he said, 'Yeah? And what can I do from here?' And they were like, 'Well, sir, she has a little boy with her, and we want to know if you gave her permission to take him?' And he went, 'Funny you should say that, because I didn't know anything about it.' They just said 'Thank you' and hung up. That was the end of the conversation.

After about four hours, I'd had enough. I said to the customs people, 'Fine. Put us on the plane. Let's go,' and my son suddenly said, 'Wait a sec, Mum.' And then my son's dad called me back. I put him on the phone to the customs people, and they let us through.

Toronto was special. Wiley loved Toronto. I think Toronto had a bit of love for Wiley as well.

When we first arrived, Drake was on tour, but his producer got in contact to see what we were doing. He said, 'Ah, he's really upset that he's just missed you.' And when he got back, we saw him quite a lot. And The Weeknd, The Weeknd was there. Jermain Defoe was there, for example. He went over to play football, when he was on loan from Tottenham. There were loads of people out there at that time, come to think of it, loads. And there was also the basketball.

We went to see the Toronto Raptors a few times. He loved that too. He was Instagramming from there quite a lot, I remember, because everyone back home was cussing him: 'What are you talking about basketball for? You're British.'

I remember us going to the Raptor shop one day with my son and buying him shirts and stuff, and this man came over and said, 'Do you mind if I put your kid in an advert?' Kylea was like, 'Yeah, course, course.' So the man took photos of my son, and said that they could get us some courtside tickets if we wanted them.

They were actually meant to go to me, as they had used my son for the shoot, but Kylea wanted them. He was like, 'Well, I'll go first. But we'll take turns, we'll take turns.' And when he went, he met even more people. There was quite a scene at the Raptors at that time, courtside, and Kylea wanted to be a part of it. But I was like, 'Listen, you are not the dad, you're just using the kids to get courtside tickets.' And he'd be like, 'Right, do you know what, we'll all go together.' But the thing was, you couldn't take kids courtside, so that plan didn't quite work out. But we all went together a few times nevertheless. Just sat in the normal seats and watched the games. The funny thing was, the advert wasn't some small picture in a programme or whatever. It was on a giant poster outside the stadium. People got to know us – 'the English family', they called us. It was funny. We'd all walk in like celebrities. The fans would call to us, 'English family!'

This was before he moved to Cyprus. He was like, 'Let me try and live here. Let me get away.'

63. Letter 2 Dizzee

The only thing you've said that ever hurt me was: 'I have not known Wiley longer than I did know him.'

Why? Because if you hadn't met me, you wouldn't be here. If I hadn't met you, I wouldn't be here. That's why.

I'm still Wiley, and you're still Dizzee. We're the yin and yang of the game. It doesn't need friendship, it just needs closure.

You've achieved a lot without me. No one can take that away from you. But the reason you're Dizzee is because I'm Wiley. We came out of the ashes together and made a future.

You act like you've never met me; but imagine if that was true. What would have happened? Would you have met Nick? Would you have made 'I Luv U'? I wish that we could reconnect, because there's nothing between us big enough or reason enough for us not to. But maybe you've forgotten.

I understand it if you're sitting there thinking that I wanted you to get stabbed. But then you need to remember that we all made mistakes there. If you've got a problem you should ring me and address it. If you haven't got a problem, it's fine. We need to speak.

I never wrote your bars; I never gave you your patterns. But when I was eighteen and you were sixteen I let you drive my car when you didn't have a licence; I took you to raves; I introduced you to people who became strong figures in your life. I did what was needed for you to become Dizzee Rascal. You were put on a pedestal, and you were killing it. But then you ran off like you just didn't care, only to come back and say, 'Yeah, I'm grime – I'm the don!' Treating people who haven't done anything for you as if they're special. Acting like you don't even know me.

I can see it with some people – a look in their eyes, that they're happy we don't talk. We had a show a while ago. Bedford Park. You remember? My booking agent sent me a picture of the poster. It said that I was supporting Dizzee Rascal. And I was like, 'Rah! I'm supporting Dizzee!' I knew people would talk, but then I thought, 'Fuck what people say.' I was happy to be supporting you. To be on the same stage as you, after all these years. And then I saw the *Time Out* interview. What did you say? 'No one's supporting me. I'm just on my own things.'

It's been fifteen years. We're older now. We've both nearly died, Jesus Christ. But as much as I want to get past it, you don't know how to act around me any more because you're not around people like me any more. Maybe you can only be around people who are lower than you now, people who you can control. People who either like you, or me. And there are people who roll with you, who are actually happy that you like them – and not me.

So maybe you can't let it go. Maybe you're holding a grudge. I get that. There are people I will never talk to again too. And you know, I might talk shit once in a while and run my mouth. But that's just me, bruv.

How could you think I haven't got love for you?

Oh, you see when something happens, yeah?
You know everything happens for a reason, innit
So you know when something happens, it happens for a
    reason
You know that innit, Rascal
It all happens for a reason, just brush your shoulders, you
    get me

I know you hate me, cos of what happened, now it's all
    changed
And I'm not saying you should like me, cos I won't change
And I'm not trying to be rough now, I'm just holding it down
You know that life is messy, it can go up and down
I know you hate me cause I was just being a wiley yout
You shouldn't think I'm sick, I'm normal. I'm very real
I know you hate me cos you thought I was going on grimey
You shouldn't think that I was just showing a little love, I'm real
I wouldn't do anything directly at you, come on, this is me
    we're talkin' about

I'm just me, I'm rowdy powdy, and you know I wouldn't hurt
    you on purpose
Come on, this is me we're talking about, I'm not here for that
    purpose
And I wouldn't do anything against you, it was just you and
    me rollin' deep
Me and her, that was just some next ting
And I wouldn't do anything to stop your career, you could
    still be here
A boy is a boy and a girl is a girl, I swear

Hate is a strong word
I think, why do you hate me?
I'm not against you, I'm not against you
If it happens, then it happens for a reason
It must have, it must have happened for a reason
It must have happened for a reason

Hate is a strong word
I think, why do you hate me?
I'm not against you, I'm not against you
If it happens, then it happens for a reason
It must have, it must have happened for a reason
It must have happened for a reason

I know you hate me cos I go on every station, it's OK
I don't wanna be tied down to just one station, it's OK
I know you hate me cos you think I write lyrics
And I aim them at your crew
Come on, blud, that's not true

Cos I know who is who, and I know where I'm from
And I know I am me, and I know you are you
So you should know who is who, and you should know
    where you're from
And you should know I am me, and you should know you
    are you
You got to understand, we are always gonna do our thing
You must understand, we're not trying to be better than you
You must understand, I'm just trying to make some money,
    man
You've gotta understand, I'm not watching anybody's plans
We've got our own plans, I'm not gonna sit here and watch
    it fail
We've got our own plans, me and Roll Deep see clear
We've our own plans, don't be fooled by rumours that you
    hear
We've got our own plans
And right now, my time is coming near
You shouldn't . . .

Things happen for a reason
If we have an argument, it happens for a reason
If we don't see eye to eye, it happens for a reason
If you don't have it, you don't have it for a reason
For bad or for worse, it was all for a reason
Wiley Kat was put on this earth for a reason
We roll deep on the street for a reason
I am cold in my heart for a reason, yo.

64. 100% Publishing

Jamie Collinson

After *Playtime*, he had a lot of commercial success. 'Rolex' had worked well, 'Take That' had worked well. But one day he texted me and asked to come into the office, and we had a long chat. He said he wanted to make another grime album. He'd made a lot of songs quite quickly and pretty much had enough for the album at that point. He'd been doing a lot of recording in Toronto, in Drake's studios, I think.

This was not long after the *Zip Files* leak, so there was a lot of Wiley music out there, but it was a great album. In many ways just as good if not better than *Playtime Is Over*, and a new direction for him. More sonically adventurous. The album came together quite easily. Ewan designed the cover again, and we suggested Spencer Murphy as a possible photographer. His work is quite gritty, but beautiful. We shot it all at Ewan's studio on Kingsland Road. There was a long wait for the barber, I remember.

65. Second Name's Drama

'I'm a don. You hear it when you listen to my songs. I can do it doesn't matter where I'm from. But I'm like Yonge Street when I'm being long.'
Yonge Street

John Woolf

He's a maverick. He does what he wants to do. But there is no agenda whatsoever – it all depends on how he's feeling in a particular moment. I don't know where he would be now if he had taken some of the chances he's had, but then again, if he'd taken them, he might not be Wiley.

We'd been working in the US, supporting Jay-Z, and flown over to the UK for a few tour dates. We didn't really get to hang around with Jay much until that point, but we'd planned to meet up after a show in Manchester. We do the show in Manchester, and to be fair, we were tired. It had been a long stint. Jay-Z calls and says that he can't make it, but that Kanye West and Beyoncé are in Scotland for a couple of shows, and that we should all meet up in Aberdeen. So we're like, OK. I mean, you're not going to say no, are you.

We took a train from Manchester to Glasgow, on our way up, but by the time we got to Glasgow Wiley was fed up. He didn't want to go any further. He didn't want to meet Jay-Z. He didn't want to continue the tour. I told him to relax, and suggested we hop in a cab and find some weed. So that's what we did. But we've got no idea where to find weed in Glasgow. The taxi driver is taking us all over the city and Wiley is becoming increasingly irate. Finally, he snaps: 'Fuck it. Drive us home.'

'To London?'

'Yes, to London.'

I couldn't talk him out of it.

So the taxi driver sets off, but the traffic is terrible. It's taking us hours. We eventually got to somewhere near Milton Keynes and Wiley lost it again. He told the driver to pull over, so we stopped on the hard shoulder, and he called Janaya and asked her to collect him. There's me, Wiley, the taxi driver, all waiting by the side of the motorway looking out for his sister's car. It was fucking miserable.

Eventually she arrived, and they sped off. I got back in the taxi and told the driver to take me home. As soon as I get in the door, Jay-Z calls. I couldn't even answer.

*

In the summer of 2012 we were working on the album that would become *The Ascent*. He'd written this party tune, 'Heatwave', with Ms D, and was flying back to London to promote it before it was released.

The first thing Wiley did when he got back was go to the bank to withdraw some cash. He wanted a lot, and he had a lot, but for some reason the cashier pulled up the wrong account and told him he didn't have anything left. From what he told me, he was reasonably polite at first, asking her to check if she'd made a mistake. But when that didn't work, he started screaming, refusing to leave, making threats. The police were called, and he was arrested. I had to go and bail him out, and we were told to appear in court in a fortnight's time. We weren't sure how serious it was exactly, but we were busy with the single, so didn't worry about it too much.

We did the publicity slots, released the single, and it went straight to number one. And then we had to go to court. By this stage, we were all panicking. He'd been arrested in a bank. Even though the cashier had made a mistake, getting arrested in a bank is never going to turn out well.

The day of the court appearance arrived, and we all went together: me, Wiley, his brother and sisters, his mum and dad. All wearing suits, all reasonably worried. We didn't know what might happen.

When we arrived Wiley had to fill out a form and list his occupation. For some reason he wrote 'session drummer'. It was true in a way. I mean, he can play the drums. But we were number one at this point.

Then we were called into the court room. We sat before the judge, and he talked through the incident, giving Wiley a bit of a telling-off. He could see why he had got a bit angry, he said, and believed that a fine was the most suitable punishment. He looked through the form. 'It says here that you're a session drummer. How much can you afford to pay?' My heart was in my mouth.

Wiley stands up and puts on a star turn, describing his life as a session drummer, explaining that work had dried up recently, that he had a lot of bills to pay, and wasn't sure if he could afford very much at all. The judge seemed fascinated. 'OK,' he said. 'Let's make it £50.'

*

What a lot of people don't realise about the Glastonbury thing in 2013 is that he wasn't even there when it happened. He was sitting on a runway at Heathrow.

He'd flown in from Cyprus, I think, and called me in a bit of a bad mood: 'How much are we getting paid for this?' I explained that Glastonbury didn't pay as much as other festivals, as they gave a lot of the money they make to charity. He wasn't buying it: 'Well, what's the weather going to be like?' I looked at my phone: 'Sunny. Definitely sunny.' 'You're fucking lying,' he said. 'I'm looking out of the plane now and it's raining.' 'I'm just telling you what I see here,' I said. 'In London, it's sunny. My phone says Glastonbury will be sunny. It might be raining now, but it will blow over. The weather is going to be great.'

I thought it would be fine, but then I saw what he was doing on Twitter. Things weren't just blowing up on Twitter, either.

Emily Eavis eventually took him off the line-up, but added his name to a very small and very select group that are not welcome. And that was that. The beginning of quite a dark period for me, I have to say.

66. Kylea and Kylie

I got this call about doing something in Ibiza with Kylie Minogue. And I was up for it. I just hate going to airports in the morning.

I got to the desk and the guy was like, 'Where are you flying to?' and I said Ibiza. I handed over all my documents, everything in order. But he wanted me to check my bag in. I just wasn't having it that morning. He was like, 'No, sir, it's too big. You have to check it in,' and I was like, 'I'm taking it on.' He wouldn't budge. The argument went back and forth for ages, getting louder and louder until I was just like, 'FUCK THIS. YOU CAN'T TELL ME WHAT TO DO.'

So I storm off and queue up at the next desk along. Eventually I get to the front, and show the woman my documents, like, 'Hi! No bags to check in.'

We ended up flying much later that night.

67. Evolve or Be Extinct

Jamie Collinson

Every time he came back we gave him a one-album deal. And if he left, we'd leave the door open and have no expectations. But we were very proud that we were the only label that had managed to do more than one album with him, and proud of the albums we'd put together. He stayed with us for the next album, *Evolve or Be Extinct* which appeared around six months later.

He'd had another bout of creativity. This was when he was living in Manchester I think, at the time when he was making a lot of funny YouTube videos. Of him boiling eggs, for example. And he got in touch and said he was thinking of a new album. You could always tell he'd been busy, because the tracks sound thematically consistent, and use some of the same sounds. There was a new edge of humour in some of the songs, 'Can I Have a Taxi Please', 'Link Up' and 'Weirdo', for example. He had a lot of tracks, but he wanted it to be two discs. He point blank refused to make it a punchy record. And I actually think it's one of his best records. Wiley at the peak of his rapping prowess, although it didn't get received particularly well. It may be his *Paul's Boutique*. An album that's ahead of its time.

I don't feel like we've made the best album that Wiley is capable of, but we've made some very good albums. He's almost too impatient to make a classic album, but it doesn't matter because that's what's exciting about him. He's talismanic, mercurial. He's a compulsive music maker, and a maverick.

68. The Ascent

The Ascent, and getting that first solo number one single with 'Heatwave', was my way of proving myself. Listen to the intro on that album, and you'll know what I'm talking about.

I was saying, 'Look, lads, I can really do it. I can apply myself and really take it to a higher level. I'm not gonna get stuck in fifth year for ten years or whatever.' I put in the time and the effort over that period, and yeah, I went around in circles and changed my mind, I argued and had little dramas, but I did it all without causing an earthquake.

Well, there was that little *Zip Files* leak. But in the end that did more for me than that album ever would. People were feeding off it. My name was known.

It felt like the start of something new. I ascended and I stayed there, for once, not up and down, but up and up and up.

When I stepped in the scene I was always
Gonna get achievements on my hallways
I thought music every day, all day
Flew up to Aldgate,
Got the blank CDs cheap, I'm a traveller
Wish I was stable. Here we go, I'm at another dinner table
I've come a long way from a plain cheese bagel
Used to go Brick Lane quick any time of the week
Have you got to be living it to speak it?
Have you got to be willing if you're peaking?
Have you got to be awake when everybody's sleeping?
Getting double hours in, no sleep
In my city the solo, it's lonely
But then again I'm like, 'Nobody owes me'
It's a new door, can't try an old key
I don't get into what don't involve me
I ain't nosy

Time flies when you want to help everybody
Turn around now, look: you're anybody
Turn it round though, look: I'm a somebody
One spirit, one brain, one body
One heart, one ending, one start
Skips a beat when you hear a gun spark
Our safety's never been an option
That's why we took the other option
On the other side of the law
But this scar on the other side of my jaw
Could have led me astray, based on the case
But time was a healer, erased the waste
Erased the bad vibe. I ain't perfect, but I'm not bad mind
Every dog has a day, that's why I ain't fronting, like I never
had mine

Respectful, how I was raised
You ain't got to sing my praise
I know the Lord awaits me
So let me live for the rest of my days
Guide the lost on a journey
I told them once, they never heard me
I was like, 'Them hard-headed'
I can't be living off all my past merits

Interlude

The Ascent

This ain't a fluke, this ain't a parody
I be in the hall of fame and art galleries
Vision in my head before Amy did 'Valerie'
Gradually you felt like you knew me and added me
I am not a present, ain't nobody wrapping me
Shoulders are here, many women they love tapping me
Chatting about how I come across unmannerly
Like I'm in a bike gang, Sons of Anarchy
Step onto the track, burn calories
Pekker got me on the higher salary
Heavier riddims, I got the clarity
Nobody pushed me, nobody carried me
Search for comparisons, you're only gonna find similarity
I blaze weed, it controls my sanity
Without, I couldn't defy gravity
I'd be a floater, and you'd be mad at me
I'm from the hood and I ain't new to tragedy

6 in the bloodclart morning, you follow me
I run bass, I'm the bass odyssey, of course you're dodging
    me
For me to act like I never knew you? It would be odd of me
It would be cold of me, it's the older me
In effect, directly from the L-O-N
East side set, got bangers, got manners
But no respect for goal-hangers
Wiser the older I get
I said, nobody's fucking with the shower man flow
I said, nobody's fucking with the shower man, bro
You'd better know
Man can't handle these levels and I'm sorry, bro, you gotta
    go
Draw from the pain that I had and the brain that I had
From the days when the money was low
Mic sound crystal clear, we're like Bose
Walked in the dance, in the war you froze
My ability is a par, that's why I don't wanna use it
It's lairy, start showing off with the music
Shows you, why I lived this, why I do this
Shows you, if I'm complacent and abuse it
Got it installed in my skin, I was born to win
Maintain so I can't lose it
I don't know why you wanna question my flow in the game
    every day, man, prove it
Popping, I got a vibe that's popping
Won't work, blud, if your vibe ain't popping
I've spent so many hours on the radio

Ask anybody can most of them locked in
Popping, I get it done, get it popping
Been here for years and the style ain't stopping
Got a whole back catalogue of songs, but it's a new day, got
    a vibe what's popping
Don't get stuck, roll with the times
You're there in the past, we've grown with the times
Who do you know from the new generation?
No one, cos you don't roll with the times
I don't get blocked, man, roll with the lions
I will never get lost, man, go with the signs
When I was a kid I was in Limehouse blocks
Friday night, man, might go to the chimes
If you hear me sound whack tell me, I'll get my bag to pack
I'll leave there and I'll never come back
I'm sure of myself
You're raw in a crew, but I'm raw by myself, I could tour by
    myself
If it's shanks you're looking for turn back now, bro
I'll bust a roundhouse kick like Shadow
Straight in ya chest, hurling dubplates in ya chest
That flows without breaks, I'm the best

And I think for myself, I was born on my own
I don't wanna false friend in my zone
Tell a brudda don't chat to man, it's all right
Stay on your side, don't want it with our side
Enough of them are too ropey
Can't cope with all the vultures

We don't want ya here, you're like ulcers
We ain't vibing with you cos you're fake, bro
When I speak it's truth without hate, bro
Let me move on, step up the pace
I had to chill a bit when I got her wet in the face
Have you ever seen a devil when you step in the rave?
Versace shades and screw face step in ya face
And say what?
I'm too London, I've realised
At twenty-two I was getting texts from XL and EMI
Looking like a walking pound sign
Bait as you like they saw my cold town side
Don't rub your wins in the face of the hood
The outcome's not gonna be good
I know the real ones and the wannabe Suges
I had to take time so the quality's good
And now I'm back in the mix, back in the combo
Back with an umbrella, back with a poncho
If you got a good vibe you can holler me
6 in the bloodclart morning, you follow me

Kylea Part 3

Richard Senior and Janaya

Janaya: I'd say he's started getting sensible in the last three to four years.

Richard Senior: Definitely.

J: He has calmed down, I think. I remember on the day his daughter was born, Kylea said to me, 'I've got this.' And I was like, 'You do want to be a dad, don't you?' He said, 'Yeah.' 'All right, so that means you've got to calm down.' And then I remember like two or three weeks later he was like, 'Do you know what? This is so different. I never thought it would be so different.' I suppose he had realised that he was actually responsible for someone, he knew that his actions could have an impact, do you know what I mean? He had to set an example. And he did. He started to be more sensible. He's still a little wild, you know, and now his kids are older, and they understand that, but really, he's in grandad time.

R: Yeah, but he was kind of where I was …

J: When you had him.

R: Yeah, but I never analysed it how he analysed it. When we were on holiday, we had a conversation about it. He was asking what he was like when he was younger, how I coped with him, and we were just kind of discussing relationships I suppose, really, in general, and how they work and what you can do and what you can't do. We both agreed that being a parent requires a change. You have to change. I mean, I've got friends that didn't change much, and were wicked parents, but I think they would have been wicked parents when they were fifteen, to be fair. Because they just always had that sensibility, and that kind of pragmatism.

J: And I also think having his life in Cyprus has something to do with it. In Cyprus, it's all family. It's really laid-back, and quiet, and so he can live the family life there, and when they come to London he's protective, because they're so precious, but if he's here on his own he can kind of slide back into the fast life a little ...

R: It's definitely more relaxed in Cyprus.

J: Yeah, and so he's more laid-back, he's more chilled. He's always been honest, but over there, he's just like more – I can't think of the words – yeah, he's more responsible. He's more responsible. More grown up or something.

R: I guess that's because here, maybe here ...

J: A lot of bad memories are here. Like we were speaking this morning, because he rings every morning at five o'clock.

R: Yeah, I know that one.

J: It's the school run. In Cyprus school is seven o'clock until one. He takes his daughter to school and calls me on the way. At first I was annoyed: 'Listen, it might be seven there, but it's five o'clock here.' And he's like, 'Yeah, but you wake up at four o'clock every morning anyway.' And it's true. Since I had my daughter, well, for the whole time of actually being pregnant, I used to wake up four o'clock every day.

R: Your mum had that too. Every day.

J: Yeah, every day. The same with my son as well. For some reason I used to wake up and stay awake and he'd ring me and I'd said, 'Kylea! It's five o'clock!' and he'd say, 'Yeah, but you were awake from four anyway.' Like, he know he started bossing me or whatever. Yeah. Anyway, we were talking this morning and he said, 'I would like to live in London,' he said he wanted to buy more property here. He wanted to. But he said he can't. He physically can't do it. He's got a lot of happy memories here, but he's also got a lot of bad memories.

R: And it's nice, it's nice over there. It's a nicer environment for the kids, it's clean, man. It takes me back like, to back in the early seventies when there weren't all of these cameras and all of this ...

J: Instagram and yeah, yeah, yeah. You could actually just be a bit more ...

R: No freedom today, man. I find that life in London is very automated. Whereas before you could go and do something, yeah. You could set up a pirate radio station in half a second, if you wanted to. Now it's: you can't do this, you can't do that. And you've got to be out if you're a musician. People have got to see you.

J: It's part of the lifestyle, I suppose, but he has got this wild streak. I think he gets his fiery energy from my mum.

R: Very much.

J: Like, they're very similar.

R: Yeah. I mean, I plan, I'm the one who's kind of …

J: You're laid-back.

R: Well, I wouldn't say I'm *too* laid-back but I'm laid-back, yeah. Whereas his mum's got that kind of fire. He's literally got a bit of both of us. He's got my dreaming. His mum will take a dream and make something happen in the world. But where I would sit and create and think of stuff, he would do that too. So he kind of …

J: Yeah, that's why. That's kind of why he made it happen.

R: Well, people always said he's probably the reason why they did that. That's why they call him the godfather of grime. I always say, it took the whole scene to kind of like make it work. Especially when you think that there was a lot of people who didn't want it to be a scene in the first place. When those kids were playing their tracks, or when they would go to little house raves and jungle raves and stuff, and trying to jump on the mic, they weren't getting a look in. Because whenever they were allowed the mic, they weren't just being MCs, as garage and jungle people thought of it. Keeping up that good vibe, you know. They were talking some greasy stuff. So a lot of house raves didn't really wanna hear that. So they had to kind of …

J: They were killing the vibe, weren't they?

R: They were, but then again, there was a lot of people who wanted to hear what they had to say. They just had to find a way to say it. It was a new style, you know, that style of grime. Only he could do that.

J: Yeah, yeah, yeah. It is, somehow in his ear, isn't it? Yeah.

He used to sleep in the studio, or his flat when it basically was a studio. Do you remember from all those old videos? There was so much stuff in there, so many records and flyers and equipments and stuff, that he had no space to sleep. I remember going round once and I was shocked. And he's quite a tidy person. He'd probably been tidying up for about three hours before I got there. He like lived it.

R: Listen, man, I used to come in from work and check on him, and see him asleep with the headphones on his head. He was sleeping with the headphones on his head!

J: Yeah, he still does that. Falling asleep listening to music through the headphones.

R: That kind of passion, it's sort of … it's almost sort of infectious. For him, music is everything, everything. He was listening to everything, but he would really listen, you know? Listen and listen and listen. That's a thing I used to do, too. If I liked a song I would listen to it over and over again. And especially when I was making music as well. I remember your mum used to come over and give me a nudge, and say, 'What are you doing?' And I'd say, 'Just listening to this song. I'll play it just once more, once more.' And then you look up and it's two or three o'clock in the morning. But that's a different kind of listening, when you know you've got something, you just want it to be perfect …

J: It wasn't just grime, either. A lot of people would say to me, 'Oh, you know you just listen to grime all the time,' and maybe some people do, but he doesn't. At home he'll listen to anything.

R: Yeah.

J: It's kind of switching into another mode. Maybe that's how you cope with the shows, with being in the studio all day. Like, grime is shouting. It's high energy. So at home he listens to other things. You can't be high energy all the time.

R: He's always had quite a wide taste in music. I used to have CDs upon CDs, all of that, you know. We used to listen to a lot of different things. Omar, Johnnie Gill, you know. And my mum's music and her mum's music – I listened to doo-wop, from doo-wop right the way up.

J: I remember listening to that.

R: And he's good at trying new things. He's curious. I think that is the key to success in some ways. Not being narrow-minded, or fixed in your ideas. Always looking out for what's new. Having an openness. And not only that, he can tell when something's hot. He's good at recognising talent. He can look beyond hype, or what anyone is saying about a person, or how they carry themselves, and just concentrate on what they're saying.

J: Yeah, he's good like that. He's curious, but he's also restless. It's like he needs the new thing.

R: He gets bored quickly. Like me.

J: He can't sit still. It's like with the *Zip Files* – he had all this new music that he just wanted to see out in the world. He couldn't wait for the label.

R: Well, the thing about that was, his way of doing things and the industry way of doing things are completely different. Kylea's music is more of a hustle, more on a road tip. It's like it was with the white labels. His mindset is: 'Yeah, I'm gonna make this, press this, I'm gonna get it out Thursday, Saturday it's gonna be sold, I'm gonna get the money, I'm gonna put the money back into it.'

J: He had a lot of money in those days as well, so he was more into the music. He just wanted people to listen.

R: But the label didn't want him to let go of those goods.

J: I suppose that was more of a disagreement with the label, more than anything, but he is impatient. He doesn't have time to waste.

R: He's that ten-minute man; I'm that ten-minute man, too. I'm focused for the ten minutes that we're here, and if you were to say to me, 'Oh Rich, do this for me,' I would do it. But if we left it for a week, I might not. My head's somewhere else.

J: Yeah, yeah, it's the here and now.

R: Yeah, yeah. Very much. And I'm like that. If I bumped into someone and they said, 'Let's have something to eat,' I'd be there. If I bumped into someone and they said, 'Let's go for something to eat next Wednesday, six o'clock,' you won't see me.

J: He lives in the moment.

R: Yeah, he's a moment man, and musically he's a moment man as well, because you can never ... It's like you can hear something and you've got it but if you don't get it then it's gone. It's gone. As good as it is, it's gone. So you have to find a way of kind of getting it. So the sequencing was a good way of me putting something down so that I could keep it. It wouldn't have to be too precise or anything, just an idea, enough to allow you to work it up into something more real.

J: That's why he records everything on his phone. Like a dictaphone. I remember when my phone broke and he gave me his, and there was like thousands, thousands of recordings on there, lyrics, bits of melody. I first noticed it properly when we were in Toronto. We'd be walking past something or he would hear something and you'd suddenly see him spitting into the phone. I'd be like, 'What you doing?' And he'd say, 'In case I forget, in case I forget.'

R: We do that all the time.

J: Or if he hears a sample of something he likes, he'll record it, and that's all he needs. From that he can create a bass line, create the drums, create the guitar. He only needs to hear that little bit and he can create the rest of it.

R: Anything, anything. I would hum a tune and record it to make sure I didn't lose it.

69. Black Boys

I'm not really a criminal. If you asked the police now, they'd say, 'He's a headache, but he's not done nothing.'

What I've learnt is that it's not just about the police force, but the people who hide behind them. The people who control them. It's all dodgy.

I watched a documentary called *13th*, by Ava DuVernay. So I know. I know that weed is just a plant, but guys are getting arrested for it and locked up for twenty years. I know that the police system is one massive facade. It's a business because the country is a business. The prison system makes people money. It comes from a very racist background – the legacy of slave owners is very much a part of the police. It hasn't changed. Power. Families. The 5 per cent who don't wanna be with the rest of us. The people who went around the world colonising and killing, doing all kinds of shit to fuck us all up, that's the bigger picture behind the law. And I can see it now.

They can't trouble me or touch me any more. But before, I was naive, I'd be standing around with a tens of weed in my pocket, and the police would come round: 'What have you got? What are you doing? Reh reh reh.' We couldn't run, we couldn't hide. We got caught.

Police stuck on an island get bored, and they want to fuck with you. I used to have warrants and all kinds of shit. Lots of that was to do with the pirate radio thing; they raided my house. Me and the police don't have anything to talk about now – I can walk anywhere. I can go anywhere. But had I kept my young, ignorant, black-boy-council-estate brain I would still be getting arrested.

Now they call round, they can't do shit. I'm not gonna have that bag of weed on me. You've got to know what you're doing; there's no point moaning at them because they're in play already. I know what they're here for, that the people in power are never gonna remove them, so I learnt how to avoid them.

Without music, my life would have gone in a totally different direction. I was a drug dealer. I don't glamorise it because I know it's not right – to give people poison, to sell them stuff to put in their body that's killing themselves, it's not good.

But it wasn't the law that taught me that. You've got to be *human* to know right from wrong. Everything else is just gaff, it's just what you're programmed with so that people are divided. For this group of people to not like that group of people. If you're human, if you've got a *heart* and blood pumps round your body, then you're already there. That's all I want: not to be above you, not to own you, just to know – are you human?

70. Industry

'I used to go and get what I'm given
Now I go and get what I'm worth.'
Can't Go Wrong

If you come in the game now, you don't need a label.
Get your song. Press it up. Put it out. If you know that
you can sell, and you're not scared to deal with things
yourself, then just do it. If you come through and you
pop, you don't need to sign. You can see that Stormzy
did it, and Skepta did it. And why not.

If you do sign, that's fine. There are people who are
meant to be signed, but I'm realising now I'm not really
one of them. You're either a boss or an artist. I think I'm
only a boss of myself. I was just about get in there, do
the job, get the money. The label gets paid loads, I get
paid my bit. They just want you to get on with it. What
I'm really doing, is trying to earn this money and put
it back in. They don't want to do that. Any record label
wants to sell what sells. Saying that, I can go to any
label now and have a good conversation, leave peacefully.
Because I've got a good heart.

A lot is demanded of artists now. Twitter's dangerous. If you're on Twitter, and you're going a bit wild, you can say the wrong thing and offend people. What you say will be held against you. You think that Twitter is your world, and everyone is with you, but they're not. Even though some of the stuff on there is funny, a lot of it isn't. It's good for promoting music. It's good to have a connection with the fans. It's a tool like any other. But you've got to use it correctly.

71. Pick Your Battles

Flow Dan

Wiley's always had people who aren't particularly
supportive of him. He was easy to single out. It wasn't
because of his fame. It was personal issues. He's
inconsistent. People felt disrespected. That might have
something to do with it. But we were young. It could
have been girls. It could have been loads of shit.

I'm quite decisive. If someone asked something of me,
or asked to come along to the studio for example, I'd just
say no straight off. There might be a possibility, but I'd
rather just say no than for there to be any expectations
or misunderstanding. Whereas Wiley would just say
yes without checking. I don't really care if people accept
me. But he does. It's weird, because he created the
grime scene. Which was basically him going left when
everyone else is going right.

Luckily we knew how to deal with battles. We used
to watch people clash, in the nineties. They would say
this and that, 'Your mum and your dad ... Everyone
dead ... ' And afterwards you go your separate ways, all
in good faith. Because of clashes, I didn't lose my head
when battles were happening. But some people might
say something about Wiley on a track, and he would say

something about them on a track, and rather than just leave it they would come straight down to Bow and try to find him.

Because Wiley doesn't back down, it's easy for conflict to find him. He's not a person to run. He's not a person to hold back what he thinks. It's quite easy to get into stuff with Wiley. I think the champion should pick his battles. He should survey what's happening and decide who's worthy. Not argue with some idiots. But all of it adds to who he is. If he was plain and simple, he wouldn't be Wiley.

72. Studio Rats

When it comes down to it, I'm still the same kid who jumped out his cot to play cardboard drums. It's making music that drives me.

I'm one of the only MCs who recognises that the mic is an instrument. Into the cage, into the sequencer, into the computer – it's not just a device, it's an art form. I've got a lot of songs that I've never released which are just trying different things with the mic, very experimental kind of stuff. I've had ideas for whole songs just using the mic, my voice and nothing else. I'm not just an MC in that way, I'm a musician.

It comes from being a kid: tapping on things, messing around, getting reactions. I've never not created music. It's very hard for me to imitate, but innovating comes naturally. Go back and listen to 'Know We': it comes from just trying a bit of this and that on the violins. You create a riff that's yours and you run with it. Just like Beethoven.

I can't be the kind of person who looks at the charts and goes, 'Let's sample a number one smash!' It's just not in me to do things that way. That's just karaoke. I realised that I was giving producers like Mark Ronson, even Timbaland, far too much credit. I love Mark

Ronson, but he's a cover band. He just replays it all and sells loads of units.

I don't really like the fame, or what comes with it. Music is my home. I'm a studio rat. But to sell records, you need to be outside of the studio. They always say, sometimes you've got to do what you don't want to do. And that's how you learn. But the studio is the place where I feel safe. I feel happier than when I'm on stage. I'm in there every single day, like it's my nine-to-five job. It's been my job since I was eighteen. And if I can't make it in for whatever reason, I'll set up a laptop and a load of snacks on the kitchen counter – doesn't matter if it's my house or not – and work there for eight straight hours. More and more, when I step in the booth nowadays, it's not for the pain or the love. It's to feed my children. I love it, but I feel the same way a lawyer or an accountant does when they're going to work. I don't even think any more: stepping into the booth is like riding a bike.

Working is good, but you need to know you're working on the right thing. I've got bundles of unreleased material. Janaya always tries to download it onto her phone when I visit; I wait till it's all nearly transferred over, then yank the cable out. But that's just to wind her up. When something's really good I'll email it to her, and ask for her opinion.

*

I go to the studio every day, but it's not always in aid of me. Especially back in the early days, Wiley wasn't always making music for Wiley. It wasn't always for me. It's easier in some ways if it's for someone else. We get together, have a little drink and a smoke, see what happens. To create for myself, I need to turn inwards.

73. Nowhere

Nowhere is my home. Because I never had a family that made a home. My sister Janaya is the only one that I can really connect with.

I haven't lived in London for years. Every time I'm there, I panic when it gets to ten o'clock at night. I might have a million places to go, but at ten o'clock I feel like I need to get out of the country. Nothing is there for me, except work. I go to hotels, but that feels like a waste of money.

It's because there's nowhere in London that I want as a home. My mum, my dad, all these people might live there but my spirit won't let me ring them up and ask if I can come over to stay. And even if I stay with them, with my mum or my dad, my sisters or my brother, I'm not at home. I'm at *their* home.

I can't wait to leave London. Number one is that I'm black, and this is not a black man's country. And number two, the money that they charge you for everything you need to have a family, to have a home – just to *live* – is absolutely ridiculous.

It's not worth my while. It doesn't matter if I've got the money or not, or if me and my mate bought a house ten years ago, or whatever. What matters is that whether it's £490,000, or £600,000, the property that you get is not gonna be value for money. Why should I pay that much for an ex-council flat somewhere where it's cold? I wouldn't be smiling if I paid half a million for that. I'd be smashing my head off a wall. Obviously I could go to Blackburn, or the poorer parts of England, but why would I do that if I can get a four- or five-bedroom villa with a swimming pool and dah-di-dah somewhere else!

There's a big world out there. I know where I'm from, I know I was born here, but this is not my country. I'm trying to raise my three kids, so I'm not gonna do it in a place that's trying to rip the hell out of me. I want to do it in a place that's nice, and sunny, and value for money – and I feel happy.

I feel like a walking job most of the time – I fly in, I do the work, I get my money to feed my family. I was in Manchester to see my friend Wrigley the other day. *Godfather* had come out, I didn't have any bookings, we were just chilling. His studio is a really cool place, like I'm not gonna bump into someone there I just don't want to see. But I had to sit him down and say, 'You know what, brother, at times like this – and always – I just want to be around no one.' Even Wrigley – he's my friend, he doesn't judge me, he doesn't hate me for this or for that – I can't be around him.

I can't think straight around a million people. Everybody thinks that they're someone, or wants to be someone, and I can't feel like I'm at home. I need to buy a hotel room. I want to be nowhere, so no one can pinpoint me. It comes from growing up and people are wanting to rob you, to kill you, to extort you. Being famous is the same. You're hunted.

Where do we belong? In black communities, in countries that are not black, black people have to go a certain way to get to where they want to be. Think about the fifties and sixties – Teddy boys chasing black boys with a knife, saying 'Fuck off, you black cunt' or whatever. You go home after all of that, you've been oppressed, you feel like shit, and you're thinking to yourself: 'How do we get through all of this? How can things change?'

Times do change, but what's been held in over all these years doesn't. What this race thinks about this other one. We black boys should have been sticking together, like the Asian boys did. Let's go to America for a second. Look at Suge Knight and Vanilla Ice: Suge was a security guard that everyone was scared of, for obvious reasons, and he connected with the top white boy to get himself up. He felt like he was the don over everyone else. It created conflict.

When Africans came to England, there were West Indians looking at them like they're not black. How can a black person look at another black person in England and say, 'What are you doing here?' It doesn't make sense! The last thing black boys should be doing in

England is killing each other. Society programmes it in – the drugs, the fact that you ain't got nothing forces you to roll with someone to get something, all that kind of shit. But it can be different, like if I know that you're my brother, why would I throw a punch at you, let alone pull a knife or a gun?

Cyprus is a great place to raise kids. There's sunshine, my daughters can go to school without boys hounding them down on a bus about 'Gimme your number.' But *my* home is Nowhere. I've got my properties, I've got my bank cards, and I go where I can't hear anything. I'll buy an island and call it Nowhere. Get some electricity on it, and start flexing. You know why I think that is? Because me and my people shouldn't be here, we should be back in Africa. And we're not. We're scattered across the earth.

74. Turning Up

I don't know anyone who's been doing this since 1999.
I don't know anyone who will help everyone like I
help everyone. I don't know of anyone with the same
responsibilities. I've scattered myself. Everyone wants
something from me. Everyone is angry. Everyone makes
demands: 'Wiley, do this', 'Wiley, do that.' One human
can't do everything.

And what if I've had an argument with my girl? What
if I get in a beef? What if I'm cut? These things happen.
I've been through a lot. I could be dead. And these
things bother me, but I have to pretend that they don't.

When I started to come through I used to get calls
and messages. Gangsters, you know. Proper old-school
gangsters asking me to send them a grand or two. They
wanted a piece of it, and there wasn't really anything I
could do. I'm not a grass, so I couldn't go to the police.
I had nothing. And these people had everything. They
knew where I'd be, at what time. They could kidnap me,
do anything to me, really. They put fear into my soul.
I did one show at the Palace Pavilion and got stabbed.
After that I thought, 'If you get threats, listen.'

And also, I change my mind, you know? People change
their minds. Or I might say I'll do something, but life

occurs. I'm maybe too much of a yes man. I know too many people. When you meet someone good, and they say, 'Give me your number,' you say yes. And that's the par right there.

When I first started, I wasn't getting much for shows. Working with promoters who didn't care if I lived or died. The number of dances I went to, and saw things happen, or get rushed. Or take universities. I got in a lot of trouble for that. But I like universities! What I don't like is people who don't understand that you are human, and life takes place.

There's a flip side. People hate it, but if I did turn up, people would be disappointed.

But my spirit only does what it wants to do.

75. Scars

When I meet a girl, I know I have a scar on my face. It might be five minutes, it might be ten minutes, but I know she's gonna ask me about it. If she's a girl who I can get on with, she'll listen to the story, and then we move on. But if it's a girl who isn't open-minded, then that's where the conversation stops. If a scar is on your face, there's no hiding from it. I just pretend it's not there most of the time. I'm never the one to bring it up, I just hope that someone can see, and it's not a big deal.

When it first happened, I thought I was finished. I had no self-esteem. But there were good people in my scene. They gave me support; they stood by me, and lifted me up when I was low.

People don't realise that there are long-term implications as well. Being stabbed isn't a little thing. You can't breathe. Every day I think about it. I go to the gym sometimes and I can feel it. Or if you see me on stage and I'm like, 'I'm dying,' it's because I'm feeling it. Especially how fast my music is. Obviously I've done a lot of travelling over the years, and that's contributed to it. But I'm fucking tired. I wish people thought, 'This guy's been going for years. Let's give him a break.'

You don't move past traumas like that. It's something I can't say. I can't really talk about it, openly. I can't really laugh, but I have to make a joke about it, because it hurts. Letting the people think that being stabbed put a limit on my career. They took years off my career.

You can't forget it. You couldn't even if you wanted to. If it's happened, it's happened. People know about it. People remind you about it all the time. People who don't like you on social media, for example. Give you a little reminder. You can move forward, but you can't forget it. The most you can do is live life so much that you're not thinking about it. But you can never remove it altogether.

We want the fantasy story, but you've got to create your own fantasy while you can. Right now, I live on a small island. And I could say it's paradise, for me. I could. I know that I couldn't live there for a year. But you keep the fantasy up. You've just got to move forward. You can see what happens if you don't move on. You keep going and keep going. The champions are the ones who are prepared to go further than anyone else.

I realised that every scar tells a story. If you're a man and you don't go through anything in life, then God bless you. But from where I was born, how I was raised, the things I went through before I was even an adult, it was always unlikely that I was going to live without troubles. That's my story. It's why I'm Wiley.

76. Moving Forward

This is why the Dizzee situation gets on my nerves – he can't just ring me and say, 'I don't like it the way that happened, but you know what? Cool.' But sometimes that's just how it is, and in grime and hip hop, you need these myths – like Nas and Jay-Z – in order for the scene to get built. My actions have sometimes led to repercussions falling on someone else. I understand that. But some things happened so long ago, and I'm saying that real old-school men would have buttoned it by now. I can become friends with enemies. Why? Because after years of beefing and nearly killing each other, I just wanna live.

He's done more than everybody and succeeded more than everybody in five albums. That's a guy who's never put a foot wrong.

I introduced him to his manager. And his manager showed him a path. Nick knew what to do, he knew which buttons to press. Nick saw someone who we could work with and someone who he could kind of take on that journey. But it was just him, it wasn't everybody. But I wasn't alone. It's not just me. I couldn't see how it could be me, solo, that kind of exclusive situation. Whereas Dizzee did. Dizzee knew where he wanted to be, Dizzee knew where he was going. I wasn't thinking so much about where we were going, as much as where we were. What we were going to next, but like, the next day. All of us. If it was just me, I might have become that golden, special boy. But I didn't. I looked at the whole scene instead of one person. One person is not a crew. If I'm in a crew and someone leaves, I'm not gonna sit around and worry about that one person, I'm gonna wish them well and I'm gonna do everything in my power to make it seem like the person never left. I'm not a solo artist. I always saw myself as a part of something bigger.

We travelled in different directions. The path goes two ways. You can come back, of course, but things might not be the same when you come back. Dizzee has never come back. He's stayed on the path, and he's gone far. This guy is a multimillionaire. He's got the most money from this out of all of us. He hasn't put a foot wrong. And his pockets are fat. But maybe he's forgotten.

That's the road that his manager's taken him down – he's got too much money. You're Dizzee Rascal, and you're the biggest thing. You've got millions, you're miles above everyone. You don't need to connect with people, it's like you're nothing to do with them. But even though you're the one who writes all your own bars, you are a part of people – without them, maybe you wouldn't be Dizzee Rascal. If you hadn't met me you wouldn't have met Nick Denton: the manager who knew the game at the point when we didn't, the manager who turned you into a millionaire.

I always go back to that night – when after all that happened in the night, all that happened a few hours later, and me and Dizzee and someone else have gone out there to decide what to do. And as me and the other person are saying, 'Nah, we're not having that,' Dizzee has decided to do something else. That's it, bruv. You can't be a badman and a hero for ever. I see him talking sometimes, about being upset about it. But he wouldn't get upset if it wasn't the truth. How come fifteen years hasn't blown that under the carpet? I've been stabbed more than Dizzee since then. How come you don't see that karma?

*

I hope that one day Dizzee realises that no one hates him here.

The day that he can say 'You know what, Wiley, fuck all that – let's make a track' will be a great day for the scene. Because we push each other to be better. When we compete, it's good for music.

I'm looking for it. But no one even wants it. The fans don't even want it. The new kids who like Skepta and Stormzy, they don't give a shit, do they?

But do you know what I'm most proud of? Something that I helped to make work. And that's Dizzee Rascal's career.

He doesn't want to admit this. He carries on like no one did nothing for him. Someone said to me the other day, 'He doesn't like you because he thinks you try to take too much credit.' I found that funny.

Because had I not met him, he wouldn't have been with the manager that he's with now. Obviously he's Dizzee, and he's got that talent, but he needed a manager that could walk in and out of everywhere – and that was my manager.

I am a part of why he's Dizzee, and he's a part of why I am Wiley. Those are the real elements of who we are. That's something to be proud of.

I want to tell him, 'Take a look around and see who rates you! Those are my dons. Look at all the people you holla to work with, like Skepta and Jme and BBK – that's my team!'

He doesn't want to face up to that. Just like I didn't want to face up to my responsibility with what happened in Ayia Napa. But I had to, because he came there with me, he was under my wing. He was a young boy then, reckless, and I was like twenty-one or twenty-two – smoking a lot of weed, trying to keep everyone calm – it shouldn't have escalated.

I want him to know I take responsibility, because I didn't listen to the manager and I took him with me. It's not about blaming ourselves, it's just about growing up.

It's about moving forward.

77. In From the Cold

We grew up with a very negative attitude, and it continues on to this day. All the arrests, all the suspicion, all the violence just builds up and it makes you feel very cold-hearted inside. You end up just thinking, 'Fuck this. Fuck everyone.' At a certain point you just want to focus on yourself and what you're doing, and not get involved in everyone's dramas.

Making music is my therapy.

Eski, igloo, ice, cold – that all comes from my childhood. The pain, the isolation, the frustration. Some of my music represents being in a dark place. You can listen to something and hear that I was feeling that way, but the next day I might have been feeling cheerier. I'm onto the next one. The piano might sound warmer. Or I might spit like I just won the lottery. There's something uplifting in the cold, too.

My sister Janaya understands; from when we were kids, she's always been in the igloo with me. When I make music the weight comes off my shoulders. It's like I'm not alone with the pain any more. Which was the whole point of creating this scene. It's for people who grew up like me to find themselves.

78. Normal Life

'To the fans who know, I see ya.
When I started I had a heart in my chest cold like a freezer.'
Wise Man and His Words

You can't live a normal life. I love fans, don't get
me wrong, but sometimes I can't talk for too long.
Sometimes I've got other things going on. I missed
the birth of my first child because I was getting
mobbed outside. They couldn't understand why I had
to rush off.

I'll give you another example. I was outside London
Bridge station having an argument with my sister.
We're arguing in the street, we're kind of you know,
der, der, der, der. And then this guy's come up and
says, 'You're Wiley, ain't ya?' So I said, 'Look, I've just
come down from Birmingham, and I'm trying to speak
to my sister.' He said, 'Could I just have one minute?'
He's pulled his phone out and he starts playing me this
recording. Janaya's just standing there, and I'm just
standing there, waiting for this guy to finish so that I
can continue the conversation. This recording must have
lasted about half an hour.

Saying that, I sometimes bring it on myself. I remember meeting Janaya and her son in east London once, Shoreditch or somewhere, and I was hungry, so I said, 'Come, let's get something to eat.' I was wearing a tracksuit and cap pulled low and thought that I wouldn't get recognised. But we couldn't walk down the street – people kept coming up to me, patting my back, shaking my hand, stopping to talk. It was nice, but we were just trying to find a restaurant. More people kept coming – the schools must have just got out because all of a sudden there were kids everywhere. We couldn't move. After about twenty minutes we managed to sneak down a side road, and I looked at Janaya like: that was mad. She started laughing: 'What do you expect? You're wearing a Nike tracksuit and cap with "WILEY: GODFATHER" written all over it.' It was a present from Nike – a special one-off. I'd completely forgotten about it.

Fans of music today are hard to please, which is a very good thing. It forces you to strive. You can't be lazy. For years, the whole industry was systematically trying to shove things down their throats, trying to programme them. But now, they're able to decide themselves.

I suppose I've never really touched that fan base of like the Beyhive, or Team Drizzy or what have you. I can only imagine how crazy it is for them. Those kinds of fans want your whole life – I know it, cos I've been a fan myself! So even if a fan is going mad with me, I can still be human and appreciate it, because I understand it. I've never come across a fan who I couldn't work with in some way.

In England, you've got four different generations who are listening to the music now. And after twenty years in music, people aren't looking at me as an artist any more. They'll come up to me and appreciate me for what I've done, even if they don't like grime. I don't have to have a song in the charts to be the godfather.

79. BBK

'BBK got a lot going on'
Can't Go Wrong

I'm not just looking at music any more. I'm looking at anything that helps to extend who I am, and what I do. Skepta explained it to me: there's money in music, but new avenues will open for you if you're in entertainment. I was naive, so I didn't get into fashion when I should have, for example. I was what society made me, so I was too ignorant to really appreciate it. I was busy being that black boy from the hood, trying to keep it real. I wasn't open-minded enough.

The other day I was minding my own business, then I see Skepta at Fashion Week! Tinie Tempah and Rita Ora were doing it, and Skepta clocked it, so he met up with the people who helped them. I had a look at the figures, and I realised that there's more to be made doing the magazines and the shows and rah di-rah di-rah di-rah – they take your image, spread it to new audiences, and you get paid for it.

Rita and Tinie might not be my favourite musical people, but I respect that they knew that they were gonna do entertainment. With Rita, they tried to Rihanna her. She's probably sitting there and looking at what's to be made from this *Vogue* cover, or that thing with Jay-Z and Roc-A-Fella. And I used to look at that and think that meant they didn't love the music as much as I do, that they went left to do a quick fashion thing. But now I use my brain. I think, 'Why are we smashing our heads off the wall when Tinie and Rita are not?' There's money in different places.

Skepta reminded me of something that I already knew, because when I was four years old I was at Fashion Week! My uncle Ian used to take me every year. So Fashion Week wasn't anything new, but here's me years later standing up like I don't know what Fashion Week is.

Fashion just goes around in circles. Let me tell you the truth: I might not be Pharrell, but my brain knows when something is going to come back around. Wrangler jeans, Doc Martens, Levi's, Moschino, Iceberg, Versace – it's always going to come back around, and I knew it first. When I had garms, Tinie Tempah never! That's the joke.

*

There is something special about that family. I think some parents instil it in their kids, and some don't.

I look up to Skepta because of his free spirit. He's taken it to a different level without the engines that usually get you there – no major label, no manager, no 'someone who knows someone'. You don't take the path he did without it being organic – the people actually have to like you to connect with you. He's travelled a lot, done a lot of shows, worked hard. He went and did big shit, like he went in Central Park and just started spitting. And that's why I respect him – he had the hunger and the pain at the right time.

But you can't big up Skepta and forget about JME – he's equally powerful. I don't think Skepta would be here without him. No one really sees just how much JME has to do with Skepta's success, maybe because he's the younger brother. He's so content in his own skin. He doesn't worry about chart positions, or needing the money, or even the music industry as a whole.

I remember buying the *Guinness Book of Records* and it had Pay As U Go charting in there. There's a part of me that always felt, even as a kid, that I wanted to be a star. But JME didn't care about positions, and stars, and all that bullshit. He knew that he was a man, different. Things don't gas him; he doesn't hear some R & B then go blind tune with R & B melodies. He's very into what he does. He's got integrity. He's straightforward grime and that's what I respect him for.

80. The King's English

I'm not allowed in America, and that's the one place I've always wanted to go back to. That's a pain.

I'm working on it now, but it's taken years to fix. And do you know the reason? Not for anything serious, or stupid, but because I didn't pay tax. On my way out, they stopped me, and said, 'What have you been doing here?' So I said I was over for a couple of shows. They didn't like that: 'Oh, so you've been doing shows here? Getting paid? And who's paying the tax?' I was like, 'I don't really know.'

So I must have had a flag up for that. And then the next time I went, they pulled me out and checked my police record. I had one charge – for a £20 bag of weed. It was about to expire anyway, but they were like, 'Drug offence. You're not going in.' I was like, 'Really?' and they were like, 'Yeah, it's drugs.' I said, 'Come on, it was a £20 bag of weed.' They were like, 'A £20 bag of weed is still drugs.' And now weed's legal over there ...

It hurts not being able to go to America. I was too gassed. I was too excited. I messed it up for myself. You know what I want to do if I get to go back? I want to eat food. I want to go to In-N-Out Burger. I want to be an 01, alien, you-cannot-even-see-me tourist. Why would I want to go and say, 'Oh, I'm Wiley, and I'm here to take over'? There's so much energy to absorb in America – just walking around, going to shows, going to basketball games. You can learn so much just by going somewhere, finding people and gelling with them.

I have a lot of people supporting me over there. When I get to go back, it's going to be mad. Canada was a taste of the vibe. I was so happy when I got through Toronto. I stayed there for six months.

*

I don't think that an English MC or rapper can go to America and be bigger than someone who's already there. I think that's impossible. You can't go to a place that speaks one way, turn up with your accent and say, 'Hey, everybody! I'm taking over – make sure you like me more than the ones you know already!'

Think about it. The American movie world is huge. They're used to hearing things that reflect their own voices. So if someone went over there who could really spit, the general public would prefer that they imitated and emulated an American accent. They'd be like, 'Just do an Iggy Azalea! Just do a Slick Rick!' And really, they've got a right to, because they invented hip hop. Record labels try to get around this by shoving artists into people's brains but it's not going to work. At the end of the day, they're not going to like something just because you told them to.

I hear Americans talking about Drake's *More Life*, and saying they skip the UK parts. It's not because the UK artists are shit – I know they like Giggs and Skepta in some parts of America – they just can't hear what we're about. We all speak English, but we're so naive and dismissive towards people who speak a different kind of English. A Londoner – cockney, straight or rudeboy – can always hear another Londoner. So in America, they can understand each other better than they can someone from the outside. Drake can do what he does because American and Canadian English is so close, I couldn't even tell the difference at first. Each person is looking to hear someone who comes from the same place.

I'm not gonna worry about who doesn't rate my accent. I do my thing and spit my bars for people like me, who are open-minded. I like all the kinds of English – Manc, Brummie, Irish, Scottish, everything! I can make myself understand someone, no matter where they come from. I'm the only one on the scene who can stand up and say, 'I can hear you all. I appreciate you all. And when I get home, I'm gonna sit there and practise all your accents.'

I was always moving between different voices – even on *Treddin' on Thin Ice* I was talking like a geezer, talking like a rudeboy, talking like a West Indian. Wretch 32 knows about this too, because he's grown up on American rap. He's not come from that garage MC tradition, 2/2 bars and all that, he's a proper rapper.

If he had an American accent, he'd blow up over there like that.

Other people aren't like that though. So someone from London will be stuck in their ways, and not want to hear a Manchester accent in music. It tends to go that way: people from Manchester will be more open-minded to a London voice, cos they like Kano and that. But if they get a whiff of 'Rah, people from London don't like our accent!' it'll set them off right away. It puts them in a space thinking that no one likes what's coming out of up north. Up-north accents are a bit American anyway; their MCs are slyly like, 'What up, maaaan?'

England's never been first in the entertainment world. An American song gets played on the radio a thousand times, and then everyone's walking along singing it. We're programmed to copy American culture. Even the Beatles did that! The difference between me, Dizzee, Skepta and all the other UK rappers is that we've admitted to ourselves that we speak this way, and we don't want to programme ourselves to change.

We need to remember that English is not our language. Black people sometimes forget that we may walk around talking it, that we've been taught it, but that's not the language we were speaking hundreds of years back. So how can a black Brit tell a black American they're not speaking proper English? When black people reach out to each other, it's not going to happen if you talk in the straightest possible way. What we all have in common is that everyone hates Prince Charles's English.

I'm the only artist in the world who wants to hear everybody's English. I must be the king, cos I can hear every single one of you.

81. Reputation

'Money, pressure, fame, it's awkward.
They want me thinking backwards but instead I'm looking
forwards.'
Talk About Life

These days a lot is about how you present yourself. The press is the press. It's not gonna change, it was there before me with the Beatles and Dolly Parton, and it'll be here after I'm gone.

At the beginning of my career, I used to get mad at all the misrepresentation and dah di-dah di-dah. But then I got to know some journalists properly, and I started to understand what their job was all about.

It wasn't always that they set out to misrepresent me, but it was like they'd overwrite me. You meet me once a year to tell the same story, and you do it the way that the *Evening Standard* says you've got to. I can't change that game.

The most frivolous media makes the most famous people. Bad media, good media – what's worse is not being talked about at all. You've just got to ride that wave. And the one woman who's done that perfectly, and come out on top, is Kim Kardashian.

Everyone has sex, not everyone films it, but whatever. Whether it was the boy or someone else who was evil in that situation, it wasn't her fault that it got out.

People came for her with their horrible bullshit, their frivolous ways. It was like she'd ever be known for that one thing. But now people know her for the programme, yes?

Now her, her sisters, her mother, her brother – they've all got prestige. Lots of people are looking at what they are doing and wanting to copy it. I've heard women, even young girls, say, 'I wanna get this done, I might get that done, I want to have these injections.' Just to look like her! Kim Kardashian's got the influence.

6 In the Morning

This ain't a fluke, this ain't a parody
I be in the hall of fame and art galleries
Vision in my head before Amy did 'Valerie'
Gradually you felt like you knew me and added me
I am not a present, ain't nobody wrapping me
Shoulders are here, many women they love tapping me
Chatting about how I come across unmannerly
Like I'm in a bike gang, Sons of Anarchy
Step onto the track, burn calories
Pekker got me on the higher salary
Heavier riddims, I got the clarity
Nobody pushed me, nobody carried me
Search for comparisons, you're only gonna find similarity
I blaze weed, it controls my sanity
Without, I couldn't defy gravity
I'd be a floater, and you'd be mad at me
I'm from the hood and I ain't new to tragedy

6 in the bloodclart morning, you follow me
I run bass, I'm the bass odyssey, of course you're dodging me
For me to act like I never knew you? It would be odd of me
It would be cold of me, it's the older me
In effect, directly from the L-O-N
East side set, got bangers, got manners
But no respect for goal-hangers
Wiser the older I get

I said, nobody's fucking with the shower man flow
I said, nobody's fucking with the shower man, bro
You'd better know
Man can't handle these levels and I'm sorry, bro, you gotta go
Draw from the pain that I had and the brain that I had
From the days when the money was low
Mic sound crystal clear, we're like Bose
Walked in the dance, in the war you froze
My ability is a par, that's why I don't wanna use it
It's lairy, start showing off with the music
Shows you, why I lived this, why I do this
Shows you, if I'm complacent and abuse it
Got it installed in my skin, I was born to win
Maintain so I can't lose it
I don't know why you wanna question my flow in the game
    every day, man, prove it
Popping, I got a vibe that's popping
Won't work, blud, if your vibe ain't popping
I've spent so many hours on the radio
Ask anybody can most of them locked in

Popping,
I get it done, get it popping
Been here for years and the style ain't stopping
Got a whole back catalogue of songs, but it's a new day, got
    a vibe what's popping
Don't get stuck, roll with the times
You're there in the past, we've grown with the times
Who do you know from the new generation?
No one, cos you don't roll with the times
I don't get blocked, man, roll with the lions
I will never get lost, man, go with the signs
When I was a kid I was in Limehouse blocks
Friday night, man, might go to the chimes
If you hear me sound whack tell me, I'll get my bag to pack
I'll leave there and I'll never come back
I'm sure of myself
You're raw in a crew, but I'm raw by myself, I could tour by
    myself
If it's shanks you're looking for turn back now, bro
I'll bust a roundhouse kick like Shadow
Straight in ya chest, hurling dubplates in ya chest
That flows without breaks, I'm the best

And I think for myself, I was born on my own
I don't wanna false friend in my zone
Tell a brudda don't chat to man, it's all right
Stay on your side, don't want it with our side
Enough of them are too ropey
Can't cope with all the vultures

We don't want ya here, you're like ulcers
We ain't vibing with you cos you're fake, bro
When I speak it's truth without hate, bro
Let me move on, step up the pace
I had to chill a bit when I got her wet in the face
Have you ever seen a devil when you step in the rave?
Versace shades and screw face step in ya face
And say what?
I'm too London, I've realised
At twenty-two I was getting texts from XL and EMI
Looking like a walking pound sign
Bait as you like they saw my cold town side
Don't rub your wins in the face of the hood
The outcome's not gonna be good
I know the real ones and the wannabe Suges
I had to take time so the quality's good
And now I'm back in the mix, back in the combo
Back with an umbrella, back with a poncho
If you got a good vibe you can holler me
6 in the bloodclart morning, you follow me

82. Creating

I've always had a laptop. I create off-road, and on-road.
Online and off-line. I can create everywhere. In a train
up to Manchester, in a boat on a cruise. I put an idea
down, and it's down. I might not finish it then and there,
but I'll come back to it. I've always been like that.

I treat it like work. Nine to five. If you're on the ball,
you should be in the studio sixteen hours a day, then do
a show, or an interview. It doesn't stop.

If I'm not stimulated, I can't move forward. I can't
get to the next checkpoint. I've never been settled, you
know? I've never been in one place for fifteen years, got
my water bill down to £30 per month. Travelling is what
I run on. I went to Jordan the other month. I loved the
vibe. That got me to the next checkpoint, no question.
London is a great place to work, don't get me wrong. But
it's hard to live there. I've got three children. If I was
working in London and trying to live there, I'd be eaten
alive. I couldn't cope with the rat race. It leaves you no
time for anything else.

In terms of the music itself, my mind knows what
it wants. I don't think about it too much. I know what
I'm doing. It's a bit like a football player. He knows
where the goal is. It's not just me. I need an engineer

who knows how I work and what I'm trying to do. But otherwise that's it.

Maybe in the old days, I'd also need a little bit of weed. But recently, I stopped smoking weed, and I kind of caught up with myself. When you're smoking weed, a part of you is way ahead, and the rest of you is way back. If weed slows you down and stops you thinking so fast, then it can be a good thing. If thinking fast causes trouble. But if it slows you down too much, then you become a zombie. I realised, which is something I think I always knew, that my performance, and my work, and my approach are a lot better without weed.

It was easy for me to stop, because I hadn't started smoking when I was young. If I'd started at fourteen in school then it would have been impossible. Luckily I started late, and I've had a few breaks along the way.

It's like any addiction. If we look at anything that we consume that alters our mindset, that makes us feel giddy, or calms the pain, it's all basically the same. Everyone has a little vice, and that's fine. But it's a drug. I'm glad that I know how to kick it. Because it had me. For eighteen years it had me.

I shouldn't be moaning because I've made good money, but when you're getting older, you realise that the job doesn't last for ever. You can't keep it up for ever. You've got to do what you can to stay on top.

83. Long Odds

'*Pick yourself up, don't be lazy, wake up.*
Make yourself move, life is moving faster now.'
Pick U R Self Up

I know how good an MC I am. I know my abilities, and I
know other people's too. Making the *Godfather* album, I
wanted to show people what the scene was looking like –
cos it's *my* scene.

When I MC against someone, I know I've gotta flex.
The only two people in the game who can bring that
out in me are Devlin and Durrty Goodz. I know with
them it's gonna be a dangerous day. They're not gonna
make it easy for me, and it's not always gonna go my
way. It's cos they're from the streets. They know about
flows, they know how to ride the riddim. And if I can
keep up with that, people will go, 'Oh shit! Wiley knows
how to ride the riddim.'

With Kano or Ghetts we can make a cool track. But
they'll be MCing with me, they're not trying to take my
head off. But when you MC against Devlin or Durrty
Goodz, all they know how to do is take off your head.
They're dangerous because I can honestly stand up and

say that they're better than me. I know that they'll kill the tune, that they'll be clever and smart, and someone who doesn't know them might hear something like 'Holy Grime' and sit up and pay attention.

Recently, me and Goodz were working on a five-track project. But when my engineer first heard it, he shook his head. 'Nah, man, there's something missing.' In my head I'm like, 'Please don't say it, I know what's coming next . . .' and he goes, 'He doesn't sound better than you. This record is a lie.' And I knew straight away what he meant. If I'm standing in front of Durrty Goodz, then we'd get what my engineer wants to hear: venom. The danger, the malice, the drive to take someone's head off.

It sounds weird, for me and my engineer to bring someone back just so they could sound better than me. Maybe I should have just shut up. But the other way to look at it is that I chose to do this project because I respect Durrty Goodz, and I know what he can do. I want him to get to where he deserves to be, because he doesn't have all the accolades that he deserves. I can't sit there on a tune where he doesn't sound as good as he is, because that's just fake. That's why no one wants to work with this boy. Everybody is scared of Durrty Goodz. The top MCs don't want to ring him up and get him on a tune, cos they know he'll blow them out of the water.

That's the difference between a brand and an artist. I need everything to be as real as it possibly can be – even if I come off worse.

*

My music definitely has a social conscience. It wants everyone who's in a bad situation to get out of it. I want people to see a light at the end of the tunnel.

I grew up on a council estate where they told you that your life was only gonna turn out that way too. I'm not just talking about the government, but just like humans. It felt like it was natural that if you grew up on North Peckham estate that you were gonna be in prison by the time you were twenty-one.

The odds are against us. But that's what helps us to become who we are – maybe if the odds were for us, we wouldn't even be here. It's like someone says you can't do something, so you go, 'OK then! I'm gonna do it, just to prove myself to you.'

Grime is an underdog's art. Because on any given day, someone new might be the king of grime. But as soon as everyone says it, there are ten MCs looking to take that person down. So it's always about going against the odds, it's always about the competition, the battling. It's about staying current.

I've never felt underrated, because I know myself. I know my level of MCing and I know what I'm capable of. Being an underdog doesn't mean you underrate yourself.

*

You've got to realise that this game isn't easy. You've got to work and work, and you've got to have some luck, and you've got to have people helping you.

I got my first deal because Dizzee Rascal was popping. I was selling vinyl, selling drugs. Dizzee brought me up, made it possible for me to get signed. And then Roll Deep. Roll Deep was the first grime outfit to get a record deal. And before that, So Solid led the way. They were garage legends. They sold a million records. Same thing with Heartless.

I've never stopped, but I kind of stepped off for a while. Grime hasn't always been popular. When Meridian Dan released 'German Whip', I saw it returning. He brought it back, along with JME, as well. Grime was becoming big again.

People were starting to coax me back. I was speaking to Skepta, Stormzy. I just wasn't sure I could do it anymore. This was like fifteen years after I started making music. This was something new. This is not *Boy in Da Corner*. This isn't *Treddin on Thin Ice*. This isn't Crazy Titch. This is a completely different era. I shouldn't be here. It's a twenty-something-year-old's game, with Skepta and JME and Stormzy at king level. But they encouraged me, and helped me, and now here I am, however many years after I first started. I got where I am today because of Stormzy and Skepta, you know?

*

Grime is a man's game, as well. That has to change. I love any female who has got the drive to go in the game amongst men and beat them. Like DJ Wildchild from back in the day. That was my name as well, back when I DJed, but then she went on Kool FM and killed it. Afterwards everyone was like, 'Why did you steal her name?' I tried to explain, 'Well no, in actual fact it comes from *ThunderCats*. WilyKat. Wildchild. I don't know if she likes *ThunderCats*, but that's where I got it from.' It had to go. God bless her, though. She was sick. That's why she's so important to me. One woman killing it in the industry at that time, with all of the men probably trying to get onto her.

Grime's male-dominated, but that doesn't mean it's not open to females. Mz Bratt, Lady Leshurr, they've always been there. My whole career I've come across girls who spit fire on the mic. But it does take extra work for them to come through and be respected.

I've always wanted more women on the scene, cos I've seen it in rap – like Lil' Kim and Foxy Brown, and all that kind of thing. I've always wanted things to be equal. Now I've got daughters, I'm even more interested in seeing things level out. It's about time.

84. Big Belly

Maybe I could have been the Russell Simmons of the UK.

I've never really made money from any artist. I always used to think that if I sign someone and take a percentage, when they learn what I've done, they're going to hate me, and they're going to go anyway. All the people I was working with were my friends. I didn't want to make money from my friends. You do that, and one day you wake up and your friends are gone. They don't want you to be the big belly. But I suppose that was the proper businessman thing to do.

I could have easily done the Megaman thing: set myself up at the top of a hierarchy, and brought people through on the condition that I get a cut.

But as the years unfolded, I saw So Solid Crew fall apart. You'd see tweets that someone wasn't happy with how they were being treated, or the percentage of money that they got. And I just didn't want that. I didn't want to create bad feeling because I'd made people unequal.

If I'd followed Megaman's example I'd be a millionaire by now. But I'm not the kind of person to say, 'I'm the boss, so I'm taking this and I'm taking that,' because that's just not fair. I want to give everyone the same platform.

85. A Brief History of Humankind

I went to east London the other day, and I saw how
much it's changed. It's more mixed, it's got more culture,
more community. Lots of love, lots of family, lots of
different kinds of people. That's what I like to see. When
my daughters have a party, I want to look out and be
able to see people from every race. It's multi-culture for
me, or I don't wanna know.

Multiculturalism, that's what I'm on. You see in
Jerusalem you have Christians, Muslims, Jews, bare
kinds of people living together. And that's the kind of
world I want my children to grow up into. I don't want
my child to go into a world that's dictated on colour
and classism and all the rest of it. There's a difference
between knowing right and wrong, and living by rules
which are meant to keep people separated. If you've got
your head screwed on, you'll live like there aren't any
rules. If you know right and wrong, then the rest is just
writing.

I don't have the energy to do that black and white
thing. When I look at myself, I'm brown. I'm black, but
I've been diluted somewhere down the line. I'm from
Trinidad – so the Spanish have come down there and
fucked about, and there's Indian as well. I know wagwan

in my head, and it's cool, but when I go to America, and I speak in an English accent, the black people there hear a white Englishman. They don't look at me like a black man! What the fuck?

I believe that black people are the most lost race, we're looking at each other and saying, 'You're not black.' West Indians especially, in England we're dying out, or we've been ravaged by drugs. A lot of shit has gone down.

If we were to forget what happened to our people, then we would be naive. If I didn't know nothing about slavery, nothing about our history, then I would be a black white man. You get me? That's what they wanted me to be. When I went to school they taught me about the Spanish Armada, and the French, and the rah rah – teaching me, a black boy, about invading countries like it was a good thing. So we need to know about our own history, and what really happened. You need to look back in order to move forward.

We need to be strong and we need to work together. No one's gonna turn around one day and say, 'OK, all black people can have Africa back now!' We need to be happy where we are. The world is going in a direction of dividing people, and I don't wanna do that.

I want people to know that we can be human, we can know right from wrong, we can be normal, without any other gaff. When I say gaff I mean the programming:

race, religion, all that. I mean, if organised religion isn't the one thing that has stopped us being human, then I don't know what has, bro!

I know the Muslim culture, I know the Jewish culture, I know the Christian culture. They preach peace. They preach love. I want people to believe in what they believe in – but know if you call it Jesus, or God, or Allah or whatever, you're talking about the same thing. It doesn't have to be this group of people over here, or that group of people over there.

On this earth there are humans, and there are people who want to control us and keep us apart. I want everyone to be equal. So if you look down on me, or if you push me up too high, I'm not gonna be smiling. I can't be happy with £10 if you've only got a fiver.

86. E3

'E3. Stand up.'
Bow E3

I'm a happy person. I don't anything to make me smile. I don't need to do anything. Where I live now, I wake up and the sun's shining. I go to the bakery and spend a euro on a pastry, a euro on a caramel macchiato. Palm trees. Fresh fruit and vegetables. There's no hassle. I can drive where I like, park where I like. Everyone's happy. No stress. It's hard not to smile.

London is a great place to work, don't get me wrong. But it's not easy to live there. I've got three children now. If I was working in London and trying to live there, I'd be eaten alive. I couldn't cope with the rat race. It leaves you no time for anything else. I just couldn't do it. But Bow will always be home. In spite of everything that's happened there. I'll never completely disappear from where I'm from. I could still be there today if I wanted to be, but I wanted to be my own man, and I wanted to lift people up with me. I can go to any ghetto in London and show them love. I can stand up and rep for myself anywhere, but it's not just about me. It's about reppin' for my ends. I may have moved, but I'll never fully come off the road. Why would I? I'm happy there.

87. Vocation

*'I remember my dad always told me life is like a game of
  chess, and you must think first before you move.'*
Checkmate

Richard Senior

He was never going to be a businessman, I don't think.
He never said to me 'I want to be a lawyer' or 'I want
to be a doctor', or even 'I want to do this' or 'I want to
do that', really. He didn't express a serious interest in
anything other than music. Music was something that
occupied him from a very, very young age.

I remember seeing a big poster for a Ludacris tour,
'Word of Mouf' I think, and it had his name on there. I
remember walking into a Pay As U Go birthday bash,
and there was this massive crowd, with Kylea on stage.
People would say to me, 'Your son's playing Victoria
Park!' 'Your son's doing this, your son's doing that!' I
remember picking up the *Guardian* and seeing his name
in there for the very first time. I kept those newspapers.

It's more than a vocation, without question. It's
his way of expressing himself. He's a storyteller. His
songs describe what was happening to him at the time
the song was written. If you listen to his lyrics, you

can hear it. There are layers of meaning in there. It's not just 'Go to the club, do this, do that'. Each song speaks to a particular moment in his life. To what was preoccupying him. I listen to his lyrics today and I know exactly what he's talking about. Partly because I can understand the story he's trying to tell, at a surface level, but also because I can remember what was going on at the time.

And he loved the art form. He loved putting it all together – the beats, the melody, the lyrics. It was always something he could see, something he could make work in a way that not a lot of people can. When he first started having a go on my equipment, I wasn't expecting much at all. I wasn't expecting him to be perfect, I just wanted to see him arrive at the end product, to get to the point where I could say, 'Right, OK, well now it's making sense.'

It's a bit like working with musicians. Say you have a band with no bass player, but you've got a spare person sitting in the corner doing nothing. So let's get that person, and keep it as simple as we need it to be, but let's get them to do something, let's put that piece of the puzzle in to hear what can be made. And what can make it better? What's the end product? He got it immediately. And he was going further. Right from the beginning. Both in making music, but also in terms of bringing people in to make it better. He sees what can be made, and he just does all that he can to make it. By any means. That's just how his mind works.

He's held himself back in some ways. He always says, 'The only place I feel safe is in the studio making music, that's what I do. I don't want to be famous, I don't want to do everything else that comes with it. I just wanna make music.' And because of that, I think he has held himself back.

But once he started, he couldn't stop. He's always thinking about music. He's always writing down ideas, lyrics. Every Christmas he says, 'Just buy me a pad and a good pen, pad and a good pen.' That's all he used to say: 'Pad and a good pen.'

88. Sunday Roast

I'm a food man. I love eating, I love cooking, I just love food.

If I was entertaining, I would cook cuisine from Asia and America. That's basically my favourite. Maybe Lebanese. Or I'd try to find out where my guests came from, and cook dishes from their background. I'll try anything. To be honest, if I had a dinner party, all the different foods would get me excited. I'd try and cook dishes from everywhere!

Because I'm from the West Indies, my number one recipes are from there. So stewed chicken, rice and peas, and cabbage. Ackee and saltfish, dumplings – that's my culture. That's my comfort food. And in England, I appreciate a full roast dinner. But it has to be a good one. They're actually quite clever, the way it all comes together to suit your taste buds. Yorkshire pudding, my god.

The best food brings you home.

Kylea Part 4

Richard Senior and Janaya Cowie

Richard Senior: He is still a big kid. Definitely.

Janaya: He's a bit like that with money, too. I remember the time when he was just spending money like crazy. Calling me up like, 'Right, we can do this, we can buy a house, we can do this.' It was fun – well, somebody that you love having so much money, it's like he was having so much fun …

R: He's supported a lot of people.

J: The last time we were out in Cyprus, he said, 'I'm going to get your son something. A little motorbike.' And I was like, 'That's a ridiculous idea.' And he said, 'Janaya, I've always wanted one of those. It will still make me as happy now as it would when I was ten.' I was like, 'All right then, buy it.' Woke me up at six o'clock in the morning: 'Come with me down the road.' So I was driving and we saw a little kid standing at the side of the road with a little motorbike and Kylea leaned out: 'Where did you buy the bike?' His mother came out, and he tried talking to her, but they were Greek, they couldn't understand a word we was saying. Eventually he made himself understood – pointing at the bike. And she was like, 'Oh, oh, straight.' I remember all she could say in English was 'straight'.

R: Yeah.

J: So we carried on down this straight road for miles. And then we saw the shop. He bought one for my son and we put it in the back of the car. He was so happy.

R: And the kids are very good with those bikes, man. Very, very good.

J: They've all got quads out there, yeah.

R: It's the thing I guess in Cyprus.

J: Yeah, his daughters have got quads, buggies. He bought his daughter a house. Actually, he bought them one each. Because their school is in the city, they spend the week there, and then go out into the country, or near the beach. They'll go stay there on the weekends. They've got a good life.

89. Stamina

Janaya

Wiley's been around for a long time, and I think the main reason why is that he's good at reinventing himself. Not a lot of people are good at that. He's aware of what's relevant, and able to recognise when he's not. But if he thinks he's a bit behind, in a week he'd be back. Give him a week and he would know how to recreate himself and he would have the music to back it up. He knows exactly what he's doing. That's what I mean by he's always been that person to be creating new ideas.

In some ways he feeds off that struggle. If I'm honest, I think the best work he's ever produced emerged from periods of feeling like he was out of date.

It's not as easy when you're popping and you're popular. It's gonna be the times when you're struggling and don't know what to do next. Then he'll sit down in a hot country and he'll say, 'All right, so I've done this, I've done that. And now how can I come back with something different? How can I make people love me again?'

He's always creating. If he can, he'll be in the studio every day, all day. Even though he says he hasn't got a job he's always working. He's in the studio producing from nine to five every day, at least. And if he's not in the studio, he's performing. He's meeting people, searching for new talent, he listens to music non-stop.

That's partly why I think it's easier for him to create new material, because he knows exactly what's happening in music today, he knows who the new artists are; he is challenged and encouraged and forced to look again at what he's doing. Some people achieve a level of success and become comfortable. They stick to the winning formula. They stop being curious. He's never been comfortable. He's never been happy living in his own bubble, in relation to his work. He needs to be interacting. He needs to be creating. And luckily, that's the easiest thing for him to do. For me, the Dizzee period was so pivotal because they fed off each other. They were both so hungry. He has never worked so hard in his life. Dizzee spurred him on, gave him fresh energy.

90. Winning

'I tell a don it ain't funny
That's why I practise so I stay on point like P Money.'
P Money

Stay on point, bruv, cos you don't know what might be around the corner. Work hard and be the best you can be, you get me?

You know the song 'P Money'? Well, I was working in a studio in Birmingham. I had to get out of London for a few days so I'd rented this space. Taken a couple of cars up, taken the mandem, minding my own business and just flexing and that. And we're working on a few tracks, taking it easy, when P Money walks in. I was like, 'Yo, what are you doing here?' He was like, 'Yeah, man, come up here to see someone, but man had a car crash.' He was stuck.

So he went in the booth, and just murdered it.

There's me in Birmingham, being cool, chilling with the mandem. I wasn't going to be hyper, I was just making songs. Then he went in the booth and fucked it up. He was on tings. I just thought, 'Oh shit. Don't drop your guard, bruv.'

*

I'm all about winning. I don't understand why you'd do something and not try your hardest. Not try and be the best. Here's the thing, though. I'm probably the biggest diehard Spurs fan out of all my friends, but I can't go to matches no more. I can't even watch them on the telly. Because I know the team now, and I know what they do. It's too frustrating.

And do you know why? It's because I want them to win the league, and if they're not, then I don't wanna know. The club's goal is just to finish in the top five, and it disappoints me. Why do you want to come top five? Why don't you want to win the league? It should say in the changing room: 'WIN. THE. LEAGUE.'

The owners don't care, because all they need is that top-five finish for business to flourish. The shirts of the star player will still sell. Tottenham are tight. They don't spend shit. And even when we did get money for Gareth Bale we wasted it.

I've got no more faith. I don't think we're gonna win the league whilst I'm alive. Coming second, even finishing above Arsenal, isn't good enough. Leicester won the league. And if we were gonna do anything, it should have been that season. Cos now Chelsea are awake, Arsenal are awake, Man City are awake. Everyone's awake! So even though we come second the season after, we've missed our chance.

Obviously I'm still Tottenham. I'm still diehard. But there's something wrong over there – the lack of ambition. The supporters want it more than the actual club. I mean, it's cool for Harry Kane to get a hat-trick, but where's that Premier League title?!

91. Grime Man

The current UK scene is very promising. There's a lot of new stars coming up. I remember when everyone was saying grime was dead. People were wearing 'Grime's Dead' T-shirts. But all it did was flush out all the people who didn't care, the hangers-on, the fake friends, and strengthened those of us who remained. The future of grime is bright. We're looking to the kids for the new thing. The future's in their hands.

Obviously a grime MC's career is limited to some degree. The best MCs speak from pain, from when they were down and never had a fiver. That's where the best work comes from. So the more money you get, the more your music will change. And as you get older you're not shouting any more, you don't have the energy to jump around and clash. You sort of grow from a grime kid into a grime man, and a grime man shouldn't really be shouting. The grime man should keep working, earn his money, be happy, and just chill out.

That's the way I feel, anyway. I'm nearly forty. I've got no business shouting and staying up with the eighteen-year-olds. I've still got the same message, and I've still got something that fuels me, but I'm not angry in the way that I was. You can't be angry for twenty years. It's a bit like football, man, you can't play at a certain pace for ever. You have to come down a peg or two as you grow older.

In England, I'm not the best MC. But I will stand up and say that I'm the wickedest grime MC, and that I will battle anyone else who's out there. I don't need to say the names of the best MCs in England. If they're clever, they know already.

I'm tired in terms of eighteen-year-olds don't want me to MC any more. And I haven't got the energy. I don't wanna get merked, I don't want them to say a bar after me. You know what I'm saying? Like, it's not that I wanna boast that I can go on radio or go on stage with thirty man, that's not really what I'm trying to do. Now I am older, it's harder for me. I just want you to spit your bar with your mates and sound better. I can't clash. Let me spit with people from my own time or just let me spit on my own, man. I wouldn't put myself up against the new generation – not because I'm scared, but because I'm nearly forty years old! It's like saying to Jay-Z, 'Would you battle Lil Uzi?' It looks bad, for an old man to battle kids. You've lost before you've even opened your mouth. The first thing people will say is, 'Look at that old grandad up there!' I can't be having that. It's not a competition thing. It sounds weird, innit, but it's like I love them youts, I don't want to show myself up. I'd rather just be a fan of them instead.

It's changed, and it's meant to have changed as well. Now I've got a little brother and he can go in there. He's learning, he's laying down there and soon it'll be his day. I'm not that new kid on the block any more, but I can still bring people together. I just want to see people flourish.

Interlude

Freestyle

I'm a deep one, deep son, came from a deep slum
So cold, after me the heat's done
Yeah, and your flow's a cheap one
My flow's money, your fans say my words like
Drink, dance, bubble
Call that a discreet one
Got so many bangers in my Mac, when I flick through, fam
I'm dying to leak one
So many bangers I'm dying to leak one
Mic wars, I'll never retreat one
You see one, you will never defeat one
When I come in the dance, anybody try and step on that
     stage and I'll press delete one
Delete two, delete three and chief one
I'm far from done, let the beat run
Yeah, I'm all that and then some
But let me know when the heat comes

Yeah well, the heat's here
And heat I don't fear
I beat your whole clique
Nan says, 'Oh dear'
Their tunes don't last for the whole year
Next year, my new stuff's gonna go clear
That's why when it's going my way
Everybody starts getting up out of their old chairs
I got a London attitude, don't care
Don't hear, I'm ahead by so many years, since family
Crying out so many tears, no way I'm gonna be broke here
Got money for the next year, next year, next year, next year
    and the year after
Wiley's a martyr, like Shawn Carter and Dwayne Carter
But next year I'm gonna step up a gear and go harder
You know me, I'm a master, I cause disaster
Cause disaster
Anywhere on earth
Find money like anywhere I search, plus anywhere I learnt
    the ropes
I earn the rights to cop tunes any stage, anywhere I merk
Anywhere I am alert, got vision, made my decision
What I wanna get schooled by a king with vision
You wanna know why I'm so clued up?
I just tell them it's London living
It's London living
And I'm what London's giving
As an answer to urban

On a good day Freddy might have Durban
And some man didn't really hear when me and Larry
Longtime buss up the version
I don't wanna hear if man's ears are burning
For all I care keep burning
You don't wanna know about the figures I'm earning
I'm in the sky though, can't see vermin
I'm earning, you're learning
And heads keep turning
No, you ain't like me, I'm too determined
Ears burning still, ends burning still
Man better take a learning pill
Think back to the days when
Everybody started maths and English plus learning

Yo, that bash done, me I'm blacker than a black cap gun and
a glass of white rum
Three black cars, choose one, it's a black one
Young black boy, too much money in a Nike shoebox, I am
that one
Got a new shirt, it's a black one, came from a black slum
Black Stone Island coat
One away, yeah that one
I been buying garms since manaman had a OB with black
one
Got a new Versace Jeans suit with the 09 Pradas, pair of
black ones
Choice of whips, you see me in a black one

Black boys drive black Bentleys with black leather seats
I'm that one, I'm the original black one, role model, icon,
    black one
And if you ain't got dough better stack some

Was a black boy, now I am a black man
If I lost my life, now I couldn't say I didn't have one
Even though I'm on a mad one
I'm gonna never fell back, like say I never had one
I used to live life like nobody's picked me
Now I got a bank card, black one
Black man ain't meant have black cards, Bentleys
Got them anyway
Big money deal next year, I'm gonna catch one
Black star made money, black stars today
But not once did he ever try and trap one

Please don't bother cos my flow's proper
I rolled round Manny, patrolled Foot Locker
See, I'm a town hopper
Ex-brown shotter
The next show stopper
Taught Harry Potter
Invite everybody, I've never been a blocker
Youts wanna talk about that's my dancehall
This is the sweet, this ain't no tick-tocker
I didn't stop cos I ain't no flopper, I'm colder
I don't give a damn if you're hotter

Your flow ain't proper and you're a chart-topper
You ain't been higher, I'm a dough clocker
See you in the ranks where the dough gets better off
One tune I saw my dough get long
Still better than clipper, better than glocker
I'm buying on sight, you're a window shopper
You take me down? You are off your rocker
We're on a mission, when I speak, listen
Cos I don't wanna see another crime sheet written
I been slippin' before so if you hear what I'm saying
There's gonna be less chance of you tripping
Make a new beat eight bars into the sixteen-bar
Make a sub-bass kick in
Whole crowd slippin', I learnt from stick kids
First ball boy running riot on the riddim
In the charts I'm whizzin', champagne's fizzin'
If I'm in a West End club bring Dizz in
Squash the qualm now, bro, I got vision
The iPod's full, how can I not listen to your songs?
We're Kylea and Dylan
Besides that, Dizzee and Wiley are driven by money
So it's hard to say if they'll listen to each other
On TV, radio or riddims

Snatch it, ya mad, I'll snatch it
Throw an in-di-r I will catch it
Even if you lived with the title belt
It would vanish

As soon as you try to grab it
The gods won't have it
Your girlfriend's not satisfied by you
So she got a rabbit
When it comes to music Wiley's a gannet
The most unusual star on the planet
And I'm nothing like Go Go Gadget
Your old flow's had it, you can't manage
Going on like you are a lyrical savage
Got more layers than a light-green cabbage
I keep telling 'em, they keep asking
But I don't know Sally, don't know Janet
Don't chat to man about Wiley
You link them gal, I live life, I don't plan it
You better know when I'm shopping I ball out
First grime kid on this earth, I'm going all out
Nuff of them lose the plot, they fall out
It's not my fault, I'm the one you can't rule out
I got your wifey on call out
But I don't go there, told her I don't care
When I'm on the strip, whips, I bring 'em all out
Bikes and chains, the lot, I bring 'em all out
Bring 'em all out, bring 'em all out
When I come on the scene phones ringing all out
I got another brother in the game who tried to stop my work
Cool. We ain't gonna fall out
See, I just want a number one so I can ball out more
Hear my name get called out more

More, more, gonna do an all-night tour
Won't be a ticket on sale, I'd sell out
I got lyrics that straight from the heart
And you've got lyrics that arise from a fart
But it's all good though, because you got the likkle boy flow
But I'm a big man in the charts
I've got a big car not a go-kart
I've made it a decade, I'm gonna go far
Like nah, this soundboy's still alive
You could die from one, I've got twenty-one scars
Ain't gonna stop till I got twenty-one cars
For the enemies, that's twenty-one pars
When I come around, you'd better ring the alarm
Got a sixteen-bar that's hotter than tar
You're a par. I'm like, nah
I won't have a bar from a likkle man star
Cos manaman know I'm badder when I roll on my own
When you can't roll on your own in the dark
Yes, who am I? I'm the best, in England, north, south, east
    and west
You can ask anybody if I got the big boy tune on the road,
    they will tell you, yes
Yes, I got a diamond bezzle
Champagne face, I climbed a few pegs
Next time you see me I'll be on my R6
It's gun-metal grey and an 08 reg
Reg, so far from the edge
Might see me on birds, might see me on hedge

In my lane I'm so far ahead
It's unusual, but I talk to the dead
Yeah, yeah, I talk to the dead
To the sound where you thought it was walking ahead
I got one title, he's got the other one
Whole family's smiling again

Like dem man are ready for the king? No way
I'm living in the city of sin
Where you might trip up, but you gotta get up
Girls try to set up, but that's not a ting
I got haters, raters plus alligators
Plus newcomers that are going to try ting
So I prepare myself, doc declares my health
Put pen to paper, then I start writing about
Everyday life, on an everyday hype
Like every day's mine and no day's yours
Watch the crowd sing along 08 tour
And out of the girls, yeah, no lays raw
But I want five mics, you get under four
And I say a lot but the kids say more
The work rate's high but your one's poor
Who am I? I'm Will, add nine to a score
Add nine to a score, in my late twenties
Before I reach 3-0, I'm going to be rich
So don't joke about my age if you're near twenty-four
Cos four years go quite quick
See, the flow's quite sick

I gave them a bit, but that weren't enough so I gave them more

Twenty-first century holds me responsible for grime kids
    that are going on raw

You know why? I'm colder, alie. That's right

Wiley's older, alie. There's a few badman that I know on the
    road

They know me. Why? I'm a soldier, alie

I'm colder, alie. Too cold for them

Alie, them man ain't cold, they are spengs

They saw me on the ends, never said a word

Wanna try ting with twenty-two friends

Ain't twenty-two, but I've had twenty-two lengs

That still feels strong, ain't got no strength left

Forget benchpress, I'm old school like a Webley Tempest

Had one way back

Just give me a beat and I'll spray that

When I spray bars I'm colder, alie

It's the return of the north-west stroller, alie

Alie, I got family in north-west

Spitters wanna talk till they've got no talk left

When I spray bars I'm colder, alie

Catch me, KB, Riko and Gareth

Stopped up the shops, black borer, alie

I'm the black cloud, that's over, alie

No way. How are you going to try and remove me?

There's no way you were going to jack what's due me

Too unruly, I'm colder, alie

2R1 cos I am, he is, the top male being

Now when I'm raving I will bring things

Got a brand-new door that's open when I push the key in
Certain soundboys seeing
They're going to be thinking, please bring me in
Yeah well, family are family and bredrin are bredrin
140 bpm, I'm a G in
Get out now cos I'm back in Confidence Street, boy, don't
    need backing
Take your crew down, there was too much chatting
Acting like that when I put the Mac in
People got me on tracking
Impossible. You can't track him
He's 2-8 now and Wiley ain't slacking
Step on the stage, the number one track in

I told them youts it's over
See, the fire ain't burning no more, got more stripes than a
    soldier
None of them ain't individuals
Who's that girl? No, I don't know her
I ain't even got a short memory
Slewed your boss since then, it was over
I'm colder. He ain't ready yet, I'm a high roller
Heard a tune called 'Soundboy' something, ain't ready yet
Where's my little bro? Subject's delicate
Sit down. I got a stripe that you will never get
Plus I'm an older, and I'm ahead of them
Got vocal skills and swagger that them two are never
    gonna get
It's over, I'm colder

They ain't ready yet

The first track the locals had, I send the other locals mad
Locals have gotta pay local tax
Local street kids spit vocals bad
I gotta leaf of dough that the locals haven't
No, I don't roll with the local slags
If you ever hear stuff, don't be alarmed
I'm a rudeboy. I brought the locals back
I make a tune, it's a local smash
Half a box, let's make local cash
Some sell, some sell, some sell, and some sell local
But I do it, I didn't wanna do it, now they wanna try and do it
But they can't make no cool tracks
Hate me or not, it's up to you, fam, but
I'm one that all the locals back
I heard some man want to take my style
Hear it, then recreate my style
Hear me on the road, 'What's going on, Wile?'
'How you been? Ain't seen you in a while'
I said, 'Two for the price of one'
Yeah, I'm back, it's the hyper one
Too many pars try claiming the title
In this game there can only be one
You wanna run up your gums, like say you're the one?
I said it just now, there can only be one
Which dad's going to be proud of son?
Dad, check my resumé, look at what I've done
I've got an MC family

Sons of sons, we'll be rolling twenties or threes or ones
Up to date, we are the greatest ones
The country's ever had, I know it
Won't fail to show it
Garments, the latest ones
Got my own 108 Air Force
I'm a Claire Force One
I never fair force, see me at the airport
Travel exchanging fun

Eskiboy in the building

92. Football and Tennis

Wretch 32

We've got new blood injected into the family tree
with the likes of Stormzy, with the likes of Novelist. And
the audience has grown too. We've always been playing
football. It's just that one day we were playing football
in the park, and the next day we're playing in Wembley
Stadium. We're doing the same thing, but to 100,000
more people. I don't think anything super significant
has changed with the music. It's still as raw as it was,
it's still energy-driven, people can still come along and
have a jump around, have a singalong. We used to be on
the tent, not the main stage. The tent might not have
been full. At one o'clock in the afternoon. Now, we're on
the stage. We're closing the show. Headlining.

We've seen it grow from spitting in the playground,
to pirate radio, to nightclubs, to legal radio, then events
like Eskimo Dance and Sidewinder, then the charts,
nationwide tours, O2 Arena, Brixton Academy. It can't
go backwards from there. It can only grow. The ball's
rolling. It can only pick up speed.

Back then it was only Eskimo. No one was doing
their own show. So everyone had to make their mark.
I remember the Eskimo Dance when Ghetto first came
out of jail. He was wearing a big velour tracksuit.

There's a stage. There's about twenty people on the stage, a DJ, two or three mics. A high-energy crowd. A lot of girls in short skirts. Wiley is in the middle of it all. And Nasty Crew are clashing SLK. Ghetto and Flirta D. Delivering their reload lyrics, getting reloads. I was in the crowd. I didn't know Ghetto at the point. Just watching. This was before Instagram, before MySpace even. You only recognised people from their voices. We were all thinking, 'Oh, that's what he looks like!' It was one of those things where you don't realise how important it was, but it was a historical moment. And I was there.

It's a different format now. Everyone has their set time, their twenty minutes. Back then everyone was on stage at the same time. It made sense. These guys were superstars: D Double E, Kano, Bashy, Ghetts. Now, because the scene has grown, there are other opportunities. You don't need to give your all when you jump on the mic at Eskimo Dance. You can be a bit more patient. You've got your own show coming up. Fans know there are other places to see you.

You don't become as respected as Wiley by accident. That doesn't happen by accident. At times he's almost too selfless. He's the type of individual who might get a £30,000 advance from a label, and then say, 'This is what I'm going to do. I'm going to take six of you guys to New York.' Or 'We're going to make a video', or 'We're going to do this, we're going to do that.' Every pound he received, he gave 50 pence back. Sometimes, for every pound he received, he gave £1.50 back. And not only for his own career, but for the next generation.

And that's why he's loved. Because a lot of people who have come through have been helped by him, in some shape or form. Whether you were in a crew with him, or whether you had a clash with him, or whether he produced a song for you, or whether he showed someone your music, or brought you to a DJ. It could have been as small as dropping you somewhere, or as big as paying for your video. It's nice to be respected by someone of his stature: 'You know what, I respect what you do. I can see where you're going to go. I care about your craft, and what you're writing.' Having those conversations, and having a little cocky argument about who was better. Those were my first meetings with Wiley.

He's maintained exactly what he is the whole way through. And that's unpredictable. I've seen Wiley be on a song with someone, pay for the video, and not turn up. It made no sense to me. But it's just a part of who he is.

Treddin' on Thin Ice is one of his finest albums. Eskimo riddims. Even moments when he ventured out to make hits. As much as people shoot people down for having commercial success, you've got to remember that it's not easy, and it's sometimes a step towards something better. When you're an influential figure, the next generation is watching your steps. So if your only steps are to show them that this is as far as it goes, this is as good as it gets. But if you make a song that the whole country can love, that I can make money from, that I can go to Glastonbury with, or go on *Top of the Pops*, then I can do all of that and go back to Eskimo Dance. I can put money into someone else. I can buy studio equipment. You don't know what else was obtained from those records. It opens the eyes of people who don't have vision. It opened my eyes.

When you speak of a person like Wiley, the first thing you have to say is thank you. Thank you because there may have been so many talented kids who would have given up if they hadn't met him. We might have missed out on hearing so much. Thanks for creating so much, because the songs he has made have added to my life.

Also, congratulations. He's been here from the beginning and he's still here now. Tennis isn't Andre Agassi and Pete Sampras any more. Football isn't Eric Cantona. Formula One isn't Michael Schumacher. But grime is still Wiley. He's still at the top of his game.

You can't love the giver in someone without being prepared to accept the frustrated version of that same person. You don't have to love that version. Because even in his wildest moment he's still Wiley. Even in his kindest moment he's still Wiley. I hope he continues being who he is.

93. Villa

If certain things weren't the way they were when you were young, would you still be the same person? You might not have the same drives, or fears. You might not be a schoolteacher. You might not be a footballer. You might not be a musician. I do believe that you can make your life whatever you want it to be, but sometimes things are written out for you, do you know what I mean?

You change as you get older. You stop blaming people for certain things. I never used to get on with my mum, but now I'm older we get along great. Everyone in the family says that we are quite similar. That we're so similar we don't even know it.

The time it struck home was when we were all on holiday together. A few years ago, not long after I had first sorted things out in Cyprus, we had a family holiday over there. I rented this big villa and everyone came over – my mum, my dad, my sister, my brother, all the kids. It was the first holiday we'd had all together. It was actually the first time we'd all lived together. I mean, I'd lived with Janaya and my mum and dad for a bit, but not really.

So at first when everyone got there, it was a bit funny just working out the dynamics, all of us coming together, everyone in their own little bit of the villa. It was so funny. I couldn't stop laughing. We bickered a lot. Especially me and my mum – not ever over big stuff, just the everyday small things, shopping, cooking, who's looking after the kids, what's happening in London. But it was nice. We all used to sit out on the veranda until four or five in the morning talking, laughing. It was good to have everyone together, you know, as a family.

I'm like that with my kids and Janaya's kids. It's good to organise things for us to do all together. I'm getting to be more of a family person as I get older. I think it's maybe because those aspects were missing when we were younger.

My mum and dad get along great now, and me and my mum get along great, too. She's living in Cyprus right now. She moved over to Cyprus in about 2013. She came back for a little when Janaya had her daughter, but she went back full-time. We speak a lot when I'm there, and even when I'm not there. Janaya says, 'Who would've thought?' She says she never saw it coming – but then she knew how we used to fight and whatever, she used to witness it. But we're the best of friends. I just think that it is actually really cool.

94. Solar System

Logan Sama

Wiley's process is very unique. He learnt how to make
music by observing carefully, then going away and
trying something on his own. He can work anywhere,
from multi-million-pound studios to Commander B's
place in Walthamstow, which is how a lot of the Eski
stuff came about. I've seen him producing on a tiny
little Apple PowerBook G4 and mixing it all down in
his headphones. Even now he'll record in what are
essentially bedroom studios. He laid down a lot of the
vocals for *Godfather* in Morfious's studio, which is just
a converted room. Wiley's never lost that DIY approach.
He makes music the same way as he did in 2000.
He's always hungry for new sounds. He'll go through
soundbanks with a fine-tooth comb, or experiment
with the Proteus module; he'll start off playing around
with drums or riffs. He's very eclectic. Wiley's never
formulaic in how he works – he's a bit punk, it's not like
that classically trained musician thing of composing in
the same way every time. I mean, when he was making
In at the Deep End he went through a phase of only
listening to Heart and Magic FM. Wiley would drive
around listening to these cheesy stations and call me up
whenever he'd hear something he liked, so I'd download

it off the Internet for him. He'd got an MPC because he'd seen the producers from Dipset using them and he'd be in the studio in Bermondsey to chop up all those samples. That's how 'The Avenue' came about.

My relationship with Wiley has never been about deep and meaningful conversations. When we're in the studio, everyone's smoking weed and chipping in with this or that, and he might be fairly quiet. I learn more about him from listening to him on tracks. He's still so revealing of himself as an artist. You'll hear him confess his mistakes and shortcomings on a record, and that's always been the thing that endears him to people. You feel close to him. He simply can't make a track if he's not ripping himself open and letting you see right inside.

Over the years you've seen him grow up as a man with responsibilities – as a family man, as a figurehead in the scene, as an MC that's being challenged. And he reacts to all those things in his music, which is why he's got such a diverse body of work. But he always comes back to that root sound. He didn't leave the core sound behind, even when he found success or had little adventures with other styles.

I think that's why the *Godfather* album was so well received because it's the sound that he started out with, that got him famous in 2003. The fact it's his first top ten album shows that the country is more receptive now than they were all those years ago. People have grown up with Wiley in their ears, they started listening to him at ten or eleven years old, and now they're in positions of influence to celebrate that sound.

I can relate to Wiley, in that we're both collectors of music. We love hearing sick new music: new beats, fresh talent, great MCing. Wiley's always surrounded himself with passionate people. He was inspired by Dizzee's energy and motivation, and he kept himself around people like Ghetts, Chipmunk, Tinchy Stryder and Kano to push himself. I think seeing Stormzy and Skepta come out is what gave him the drive to give people *Godfather*.

I've always seen him deal with people with talent as though they are his peers; he's never taken them on as a student, or treated them like a pet project. He genuinely wants to help people out. I remember around 2004, 2005, when he brought Jme and Skepta around Roll Deep. Him and Jammer were the ones who encouraged Skepta to start MCing in the first place. He inspires a lot of love and affection in people, simply because what he creates brings so much joy to people.

He's got his faults; he can get angry quickly, he can be unreliable, he can project a lot of his frustrations and self-doubt on other people. Personally, I'm sure he's pissed a load of fucking people off, but it's nothing in comparison to the profound effect his art has had on them. And yeah, he's obviously had his conflicts with people, but Wiley's not the kind of guy to look at someone and go, 'Right, you're good and you're young, so I'm gonna sign you because you don't know any better.' The only thing he seems to get out of them is inspiration, motivation and energy. He shines a light on talent.

A couple of months after I'd started my show at Rinse FM and saw what Roll Deep was doing, I sent Wiley a text. I said, 'Look, you're a genius, but I can see that you're not organised. I want to work with you!' So we set up a company called Wiley Kat Entertainment – it ran for about two or three years. I saw that when money came in for him, he'd spend it on studio time for other people. Or he'd pay to fly other artists out to New York with him. He's always spent money on giving people chances, and he still does it now. To this day, he's never asked for anything in return. Wiley has not changed in any way, the whole time that I've known him. Even back at Rinse I could see that he's not about building an empire, he's about creating out of love for the music. He's always had time for people. He'd lend you his last £20 if you ran out of petrol.

Wiley's a hilarious guy, and a lot of the time it's not even intentional. I used to drive around with him a lot when we were selling records, during the Wiley Kat Entertainment days. We'd do the rounds at Rhythm Division, Uptown Records, Black Market.

I also ended up running errands for him because I was the one in charge of the money. He got me to buy this pit bull puppy for his girlfriend, and drive it over to her house. He wasn't there. I had a towel on the back seat so it wouldn't piss or shit anywhere, but the thing threw up in the car! It was a really hot day, and I was trapped in there with this fucking stink.

There was one time when Wiley was having an argument with someone. He asked me to come and pick him up, and I drove him down to meet the guy. Wiley was arguing with him on the phone the whole way down; when we got there, he suddenly leapt out of the car and chased him with a tyre iron! After a while he came racing back, jumped in the car and said, 'Drive!' I didn't know what was going on ...

Grime can't die as long as Wiley is here. Wiley is the most important thing to grime's survival, and he's never left it, never sold out, or left that sound behind. He will never stop, and so no one else will either. He's like the sun at the centre of the solar system. Without him, all the planets would freeze and die. He's in the middle of everything. He just burns and burns and burns, and he brings life to other artists.

Where does Wiley go from here? All I want for him is to be happy and successful, because he deserves that. He's talking about *Godfather 2*, he's talking about producing an album for other artists to appear on, he's talking about a film. His drive to create, and to express himself, is unlike anything I've ever seen. Wiley is ever present, so he'll rise in the morning and set in the evening. He's never gonna end.

95. Godfather Status

I don't think I'm as current as I would like to be. There were times in my career when I thought I might not get any recognition. Pioneers don't get remembered.

The thing is, if someone is called 'godfather', you might think to yourself, 'Oh, the old guy.' But then again, there can only be one godfather. I'm an elder statesman, and people know that they're here because I am. They're here because of me, but the bars came out of their mouths. Skepta was a DJ before he met me, but I was the one who gave him the money and the encouragement to actually become an MC. Now he's won the Mercury, he's won the Ivor Novello.

Things are happening now. Now is the time. In the south, the north, the east and west. I really want to help people get on. Self-belief. Come on lads, share. You see success, and see how it can be replicated. I've got east London rappers. They're hard and they're real. I want them to come forward and do it.

Sometimes you realise that the game isn't easy. It takes its toll. Look at what happened with Ice Kid. When I see him come out at Culture Clash in 2016, I was so happy.

And then to see Chip and him do that ting, it made my day. Chip saying, 'Nah, that's my brother.' Because Ice Kid is unbelievable.

I'm his number one fan. I think part of the problem was me gassing him. I couldn't help it: 'You're sick, you're sick, you're sick.' In the end, he probably thought, 'Shut up, man. I'm not going to be sick, you know.' And that's it. It was my fault, really. I gassed him into space.

It's a mistake. It's almost like being a parent. Being pushy. You just assume sometimes that if you can do it, that they can do it. But they might not want to.

I might be the king of grime. But it's never given; it's something to strive for. Even if 100,000 kids dub me the king of grime, I might listen to them, but I know my own ability. Even if I'm not at that point in time, I know I can try to be. In racing, they say, 'I fancy that horse. I fancy that one to be a winner.' Well, I fancy my styley against any MC. That's what keeps me going.

Grime's given me a status, but it didn't give me a career for a long while. Grime is where I've ended up, but I've done a lot of different things – jungle, a bit of garage. I have always been making music so I think if grime didn't come along I would have probably ended up doing something else in music anyway.

Grime has been good to me, but it hasn't been easy. The UK music scene is like any other music scene. People follow the fashions that are in. So if garage is in, everyone will like it; if house is in, everyone will like it, you know. So that's why I was part of that, I think. I think grime is like, it's given me a godfather status, it's given me the status that I help people, it's given me ... I'm not gonna say money, you know, because it ain't given me the kind of money people would expect, but I don't really care. I've earned other things. I didn't really earn money from grime as such but it has given me the know-how to run my own situation also. So now, like, because that's why I was actually in charge of it myself. In the other situations I had people there, but in grime like, I can't go and do a grime record deal. I made the vinyl that built the scene, so if I can't put out a grime record my own self, who am I, you know? That's where I'm at.

I am the boss on my album. I made a song called 'Speakerbox'. No one in grime has got a speakerbox. Why? Because that's not what they do. I do it. I made it myself. With the Korg. With the synth presets. With Gliding Squares. I make it grime, in a way that people can say, 'That's grime.' I make music that fifteen, twenty years later, a kid from out of nowhere can make a song with Gliding Squares and everyone will say, 'That's Wiley's sound.' That's my sound.

96. The Future

Janaya

I think in five years' time, Kylea will be doing more producing. Because he's actually a really sick producer, and not just grime either! I'm talking about the songs that we listen to, R & B. Something like Drake and Rihanna's 'Take Care', with all the samples – Kylea's been doing that for ages, from about the age of seventeen or eighteen. He can make a good pop song when he puts his mind to it. So maybe he'll go that Drake route, and become a tastemaker. Or maybe he'll step away from the forefront, and start managing other people. He loves singers.

In ten years' time? I hope he'll be sitting on a beach, relaxing and just enjoying being a good parent. But it's not in his body to stop. He doesn't know how.

List of Illustrations

1. Author's own
2. Author's own
3. Author's own
4. Author's own
5. Author's own
6. Author's own
7. Author's own
8. © Will Faich
9. © Peter Beste
10. © Peter Beste
11. © Lord of the Mics Ltd
12. © Chris Lopez/ Sony Music Archive/ Getty Images
13. © David Tonge/ Getty Images
14. © PYMCA/ UIG/ Getty Images
15. © Everynight Images/ Alamy Stock Photo
16. © PYMCA/ UIG/ Getty Images
17. © XL Recordings
18. Album cover for *Playtime Is Over*, courtesy of Big Dada. Design and art direction by Ewan Robertson, Oscar Bauer & Eat Sleep Work/ Play. Photography by Pelle Crépin. Retouching by Christopher Peabody. © 2007 Big Dada
19. © Jo Hale/ Getty Images

Acknowledgements

First and foremost, thank you to everyone who took time out to help with the book, especially Flow Dan, Jamie Collinson, Logan Sama, Scratchy and Wretch 32. A big thank you to June Cowie for the photographs.

Secondly, thank you to the fans. Without you I wouldn't be here.

Thank you to my manager John Woolf, and to Twin B for putting us together in the first place. Thank you to everyone in the industry who has helped me in any way – particularly the record labels, DJs and radio stations who supported my music from the beginning.

Thank you to Tom Avery, Ash Sarkar and everyone at Penguin Random House.

Love and respect to my brothers in BBK.

A special dedication to my family, particularly to my father Richard, and to my sister Janaya, who are the people who really made this book happen. Thank you for everything.

And last but not least, a big thank you to Hattie Collins.